COLIN DOESN'T CALL THE HELP DESK

More Irreverent Tales of Corporate Life

Elwood Scott

Colin the Koala Book 2

Illustrations by Mitch Pleasance Tattoo Artist.
Instagram: @mitchpleasance
Written by: Elwood Scott. Twitter: @e_scottauthor.
Instagram: @e_scott_author
First edition 2024. Melbourne Australia.
Second edition 2025. Melbourne Australia.

ISBN: 978-0-6450524-8-0

Other Books by Elwood Scott

Funny You Should Ask – 2022
> A collection of short stories:
> some funny humorous - some funny odd.

Colin Calls the Help Desk – 2023
> The first book in the Colin the Koala Series.

Connection Lost –2023
> A Romantic Suspense about a hacker

As Yet Untitled – coming August 2024
> Science fiction, but I haven't thought up a
> cool title yet.

Available through Amazon.

You can also sign-up for my (ir)regular newsletter at
elwoodscott.com

Dedication

Colin Doesn't Call the Help Desk is dedicated to everyone (whether in an office or not) who steps up to lean in for a deep dive, and still manages to get their job done each day without falling over...

In spite of the support of their bosses, co-workers, and the business systems, procedures and processes in place to assist them.

And to Ben, Sally and Parker.

Contents

ELWOOD SCOTT

When you fail to ~~plan~~ you plan to fail

KOALA

"The printer's broken again," Bill grumbles, brandishing a stack of paper angrily in the air.

"Is that so?" Bob the boss mumbles back at him, not looking away from his computer. He hunches his shoulders closer to the screen, partially because he's trying to write an email, but mostly because he knows that if he shows any sign of engagement, Bill will ramble on for the next hour.

"The darn thing keeps printing in black and white," Bill continues. He thrusts the stack under Bob's nose and shakes it again to cement his point.

"The printer's not broken Bill." Bob lifts his hand and moves the paper out of the way without looking up. "I told you last time. IT has turned off colour printing."

"Perhaps IT should organise themselves a bit better then," Bill huffs, two pages slipping out and floating onto the desk. "Back in my day, there was more than enough print colours to go round." He slaps the rest of the pages onto the desk next to the others.

"We're not *running out* of colours Bill," Bob sighs. "We're printing in black and white to help save the environment." He keeps typing. "Or something." He flicks a finger towards Bill's paper spread unevenly over his desk. "And you can't leave that there."

"Well it's of no use to me." Bill steps back and hold his hands up as though it's a small uranium pile. "And if IT want to help the environment so much, why would they make me waste all this paper."

"*I* like helping the environment," Colin the Koala declares, walking up to see what the commotion is about. The uneven stack of paper on Bob's desk catches his eye, and he arranges it helpfully back into a neat pile.

"Anyone for coffee?" Graham calls out on his way to the lifts. He holds up his plastic re-usable coffee cup that reads - 'This meeting is bullshit'.

"I'd like to," Colin calls back. "But it's nearly time for our team meeting." He holds up his wrist and taps his watch.

Bob stops typing and checks the time in surprise. "Yes Graham," he says with as much fake confidence as he can muster, and wonders why he missed the meeting reminder. He snatches up his computer as though it was what he was just about to do before Bill had interrupted him, and takes off down the corridor. "We've got a special guest coming today, so a little hustle please people," he calls back over his shoulder. "And don't leave that there." He points back at Bill's printing.

"Is the special guest Rosebud McCrae, the cowboy?" Colin scoots along the worn pathway in the carpet and falls in step beside Bob. "He's my favourite."

Bob looks down at Colin in confusion. "Ah, no," he finally says. "I'm afraid it's not."

"Is it someone who knows how to fix printers?" Bill huffs from behind.

"I told you..." Bob calls back over his shoulder again. "It's not broken. If you want to print in colour, you need to get approval from Senior Management, and then call the Help Desk, and then get them to turn it on for that single individual print job."

"Help Desk..." Colin shudders and wraps his arms tightly around himself. "I hope I never need to print in colour," he mutters.

Bob slips his head sideways to avoid the broken 'Safety is our most important metric' sign. "I can't believe they still haven't fixed that," he tuts. "Surely someone must have told them about it by now." He calls back to Bill again, "Why do you need to print in colour anyway?"

"Why do you need to print *anything*?" Graham says joining the procession.

"Exactly right," Bob agrees. "Feel free to join the rest of us in the 20th Century, Bill," he laughs and swings left past the lifts, narrowly avoiding a stack of empty boxes.

"Um. I think it might be the 21st Century Boss," Colin says politely, dancing around a ream of copy paper.

"Let's agree to disagree," Bob mumbles, and increases his pace to make sure he gets to the room first. He grabs the door handle a step ahead of Colin and gives himself a small victory fist pump. "Let's move it along people," he says, sliding the door open and waving everyone past him with a series of 'hurry up' motions.

"Have they fixed the air conditioning yet?" Vanessa asks turning herself sideways to squeeze through. "You know it would be easier to do this if you moved out of the way."

"Doesn't feel like they have," Colin calls from inside the room.

"I'll leave the door open," Bob says, slapping his palm on the lid of his computer to emphasise the importance of speed; even though everyone is already in the room. "Alright," he says. "Let's talk about planning— Why are you all standing?" He stops. "Who are *you*?" he says, staring at the five people sitting at the meeting room table.

"It's Sally from Safety," Colin smiles. "From our team building day!"

"I know who she is," Bob replies scratching his head. "But what is she doing here?"

"Do you want me to ask her?" Colin asks helpfully.

Bob raises his hand to indicate that he's got it. "What are you doing here?" he says to Sally.

"I'm having a meeting." Sally sneers back. "At least I *was*, until your team decided to mount an invasion."

Bob pulls his shoulders back confidently. "I've got this room booked," he says curtly, and points at the digital room-booking panel. "See."

The panel flickers twice and the display fades in an out with – Unknown Error. Contact admi8&6x#9Y^52.

"*I* have a meeting room acceptance," Sally replies, with the confidence of a poker player ready to lay down a straight flush.

"*I* have one of those as well," Bob says, opening his calendar. "And mine's a *recurring* meeting, so my acceptance will be from earlier than yours," he continues smugly, ready to drop four Aces. He scrolls to his calendar and stares at the blank space where the meeting should be.

"It wasn't in *my* calendar," Vanessa says. "I'd just hoped we weren't doing it anymore."

"Thanks Vanessa," Bob snaps at her, confused why the meeting isn't showing. "But I think there's more important things to do than discuss why it's fallen out of *your* calendar."

"I'm happy to move," the lady with the bright red face says, taking a long swig of water.

"Me too," the thin man to her left agrees, pulling his shirt away from his neck. "It's too hot in here."

Sally spins her computer to show the room acceptance, and holds Bob's gaze long enough to make it clear she could call his bluff if she wanted to. She holds her stare for a moment longer.

Colin looks between them and thinks they look like gunfighters in the wild west. The air seems to crackle, but he's not sure if it's from the tension or humidity and poor electrics.

"I'm out of water anyway," Sally says picking up her empty bottle. "We'll continue *our* meeting in the kitchen."

"Thank god." The thin man wipes his hand across his forehead.

Bob taps his foot on the floor impatiently as he waits for them to pack up. He pulls his computer close to his chest when Sally tries to peek at the screen as he's following them to the door. "Bye," he adds passive-aggressively and pulls the door to slide it closed decisively behind her. It shudders twice then jams halfway. He turns back to the room. "Why didn't you say something?" He holds his arms out. "Why would you just stand around in someone else's meeting?"

"You said we had a visitor." Graham shrugs. "I assumed it was them."

Bob drops into his usual chair at the head of the table and rubs his forehead. "You thought I'd invited a meeting that was already in progress, to *our* meeting, as a visitor..." he says flatly.

"Who can tell these days?" Graham shrugs, scratching his nose.

Bob studies him for a moment, decides not to pursue it any further, and composes himself. "As you all know..." He looks at each person in turn. "We need to start pulling together our strategy and budget for the next financial year." He stops. "Can everyone sit down please."

"Oh. I didn't know that," Pooja replies, pulling out her usual chair. "Did anyone else know that?"

"I knew that Boss," Colin raises his paw while everyone else shakes their head.

"It shouldn't be a surprise," Bob sighs. "We do it at this time every year."

George drops into his chair and rubs his chin, trying to think back that far. "I don't remember doing it last year."

"That's because *some* people..." Bob narrows his eyes accusingly and looks around the table. "And by *some*, I mean *everyone*... left it to the last minute, and *I* ended up having to do it all to meet the deadline."

Graham nods. "Yeah, well, if you'd sent us the schedule earlier than the Wednesday before the deadline—"

"Let's not get down into the weeds Graham," Bob interrupts. "My point is—" he says, leaning forward to make it obvious he's rubbing his lower back. "That I ended up doing the entire thing in one solid 26-hour block, the weekend before it was due."

"Sounds like we've got a process that's already working for us then," Graham says and pushes himself up out of his chair. "We should probably get out of your way and let you get to it."

"I *won't* be doing that again." Bob rubs his back and winces dramatically. "I still haven't passed all the kidney stones caused by all coffee I had to drink to stay awake." He twists uncomfortably in the chair.

"It's terrible that you had to work that long." Umi frowns at him. "If only we'd known earlier, we could have helped."

"I agree," Pooja nods. "You shouldn't have been put in that position at all."

"Thank you." Bob half-heartedly waves at them to stop, even though he feels he deserves more.

"Yes, whoever gave us that deadline should be ashamed of themselves," Pooja continues, folding her arms defiantly.

Bob nods, and chooses not to mention he had received the deadline a month before, and forgotten to pass it on. "It was important to the team to get it done properly." He sits upright. "And *I* was prepared to do it... Because I am committed to *us*... as a winning team." He places a hand over his heart and raises his chin to stare heroically into the middle distance.

"Do you need an antacid or something Boss?" Colin asks rummaging through his pencil case. "I think I might have one in here..."

Bob takes a deep breath and slumps down in his chair. "Anyway, as part of the Agile implementation, Andre the Giant has requested that we apply Agile techniques to our planning process. Which means we'll need to get started earlier than usual."

Colin's stops and looks up from his pencil case, his eyes wide. "Andre the Giant works *here*?" he gasps and pushes himself up excitedly in the chair. "I've always wanted to climb him."

"What?" Bob turns to Colin.

"Ever since I saw The Princess Bride," Colin looks up to the ceiling. "He's so huge."

"Oh. Right." Bob shakes his head in an unsuccessful attempt to clear it. "No, not *that* Andre the Giant. I'm talking about *my* boss."

"Didn't he die?" Vanessa asks, turning to George.

"Your boss died?" Colin stares at Bob in shock.

"No." Bob waves it away. "I think she means the real— never mind." He shakes his head. "My boss' name is Andre and he calls himself Andre the Giant."

"Is that because he's a giant?" Colin holds his paws as high as he can stretch.

"No," Graham says, resting his elbow on the table. "He says it's because his name's Andre, and he's the 'Big Boss'."

"Oh." Colin lowers his paws. "I see." He rubs his chin. "Clever."

"I don't know about that." Graham shrugs back. "Also, his name's *not* Andre. It's Andrew. When he started, IT accidentally left off the 'w' when they set him up on the system, so we all thought his name *was* Andre. He eventually gave up correcting people and decided to call himself Andre the Giant because he said everyone thought it was funny."

"Was it funny?" Colin asks.

"Not as far as anyone could tell." Graham shrugs again.

"Okay," Bob interrupts. "Let's get back on track—"

"Hello." A woman who looks like she could have stepped out of a clothes shop catalogue appears at the door.

"Sorry, I've got this room booked," Bob says and lowers his laptop screen so she can't see his calendar.

"I'm here to help with your planning session." She strides purposefully across the room and plants herself solidly in front of the whiteboard.

"Oh," Bob says, realising this is their visitor. "Ahem. Everyone..." He claps to make sure they are all paying attention. "*This* is the guest I mentioned earlier. Say hello to Linda—"

"It's with a 'y'." She places her hands on her hips, and stares around the room, looking slightly above everyone's eye line.

"Oh, sorry," Bob crosses out her name in his notes and re-writes it. "This is Lindy—"

"Not Lindy," she corrects him without changing her gaze. "You were right the first time, it's just with a y, not an i."

"Oh. Sorry again." He scribbles out Lindy and re-writes Linda. "*My mistake,* I suppose," he adds passive-aggressively. "This is Linda."

"With a y." She corrects him again.

Bob opens his mouth and silently tries a few options of how he could pronounce Lynda, differently to Linda, but can only come up with - 'Lyne-da', or Lye-n-da'. He decides that neither sound like a way anyone would want their name pronounced. "Lin... Lyne..." Bob looks over at her and gives up. "Our special visitor today is an Agile Coach who's here to help streamline this year's planning process, while reinforcing our Agile..." he searches for the right suffix and eventually settles for, "ness."

"Wouldn't it be simpler to just *create* the plan?" George asks raising his hand. "I could be creating mine right now, instead of sitting here, *not* creating it."

"I thought we were done with this Agile rubbish—" Graham leans back and folds his arms.

"We've had this conversation before Graham," Bob interrupts. "We're not *done with it.*" He glares at him.

Colin watches Lynda turn her head slowly and drill her eyes into Bob. It reminds him of the time he saw The Terminator, and he shrinks back a little.

"*And it's not rubbish,*" Bob adds quickly and smiles at her.

Lynda maintains her gaze. "I'll take you through a short refresher." She turns back to the group. The left side of her mouth rises slowly.

Colin studies the expression and moves back in the chair again. It kind of looks as though she knows what a smile *is*, but doesn't quite understand its purpose. "A refresher is always helpful." He says, hoping to saty on her good side.

"I'll skip the basics and jump straight to Sprint planning," Lynda declares, then nods definitively in agreement with her own statement.

"Can we just sprint back to our desks and *do* the planning?" George asks pushing his chair back.

"I not sprinting anywhere," Graham says rubbing his legs. "Not with these knees."

"*No-one* is sprinting anywhere," Bob sighs and runs his hands across his head. He frowns when several hairs float slowly down onto the table in front of him.

Alfred holds his hand up with a question. "Can I ask what you mean by *refresher*?"

Lynda squints over to him. "You don't need to raise your hand," she says. "A refresher of the content you covered in the training modules."

"Training modules?" Alfred frowns.

Lynda attempts a smile again. "The five training modules you completed after the original implementation launch session."

Everyone turns to stare at each other blankly.

Lynda rotates her head slowly and returns her gaze to Bob. "They *have* completed the training modules, haven't they?" She narrows her eyes at him.

Bob shifts uneasily in his chair and rubs his lower back. "Sorry, I missed the question." He winces. "I think one of my kidney stones is acting up."

Lynda studies him for a moment. "The five online modules: Agile gives you an A for Efficiency. Sprints and Scrums aren't just for Rugby. People, Personas and Planning. And Why Agile is more Efficient," she says gruffly.

Gina repeats them quietly to herself and counts on her fingers. "Isn't that only four?" she whispers to Graham from the corner of her mouth.

"Maybe that's one of the Agile efficiency gains," he whispers back, and gives Lynda a thumbs up.

"Please, go on," Bob smiles, hoping to avoid any more conversation. "I'm sure it will be a valuable use of everyone's time."

Lynda stares at him long enough that he withers back into his chair. "Let's begin with what you know," she says, still looking at Bob, before slowly turning back to the group.

Colin's paw shoots up. "Agile," he begins, sitting up in his chair. "With a capital A, is a methodology that allows us to be more agile, lower-case a, in our work."

"Correct." Lynda nods. "But you don't need to raise your, uh... hand." She looks out at the room just above everyone's eyeline again. "And what else do we know?"

Colin lifts his paw again. "Agile makes us more efficient in meetings by replacing our boring, weekly hour-long team meeting, with a crisp fifteen-minute stand up each day." He quickly glances over at Bob. "No offence boss," he adds.

Bob waves back to indicate - none taken.

"Correct again," Lynda says. "But you don't need to raise your um..." She waves her fingers to indicate Colin's paw. "Everyone can just call out their answers.

Don't worry. I'll be able to keep up." She lets out a single laugh as though she's just made a hilarious joke. "What else?"

Colin throws up his paw again.

"Maybe someone else," Lynda says raising her eyebrows expectantly.

Colin slowly lowers his paw, and listens to the clock at the front of the room tick-tock, while the team look blankly back at her.

"Okay," Bob jumps up to break the tension. "I don't think we need to get down into the weeds today," he says. "Maybe it would be useful if you could run through a few of the key concepts. To help, you know..." He waves his hand in a circle. "Get them started."

Lynda stares into Bob's eyes until he slips back into his chair again. "Alright then," she says, stepping beside the whiteboard. "Let's start with terminology." She taps her green nails against the board.

"Does she know it's blank?" Vanessa leans to one side and whispers to Pooja.

"I think that's what being Agile is about," Pooja whispers back. "You don't want to lock yourself in to too much too soon."

Lynda picks up a blue marker from the table next to the bin and tries to write on the board. When nothing happens, she shakes it a few times and tries again. When it still doesn't work, she frowns at it, jams the cap back on and places it back on the table. She tries again with a red marker, with the same result, and repeats the process three more times. "Why do none of these work?" she complains.

"You've tried that one already," Colin calls out helpfully as she picks up the blue marker again. "You can borrow mine if you like," he says pulling a packet from his pencil case.

"That's an impressive looking pencil case." Lynda nods approvingly. "Thank you," she says taking them from him.

"Thank *you*." Colin smiles proudly and reaches back inside. "Gum leaf?" He asks and holds up a small packet.

"Uh... No." Lynda scratches her head. "Thank you."

Colin politely offers the leaves out to the others.

After everyone declines, Lynda begins speaking and scribbling on the whiteboard as though she's being played at one and a half times speed.

Colin tries to follow, but can only catch snatches of words as she turns to and from the board.

Lynda writes - 'Epic' in blue and draws a thick black connecting line to a series of red stick figures. She says something to the board, and then half turns to the group. "...develop stakeholder personas and..." she fades off turning back to the board and adding the caption – Stakeholders under the stick figures. "...and User stories..." floats out before she turns back to the board again.

Colin leans forward and raises his ear as he tries to follow her explanation of three intersecting arrows making their way between four different coloured octagons. It reminds him of the time he tried to watch a Sherlock Holmes movie, but hadn't realised he was sitting on the TV remote, and so the sound kept fading in and out every time he moved.

"And then we're on our way to our first sprint." Lynda steps back and smiles proudly at her work. "Simple," she declares.

POP! goes the tuft of fur on top of Colin's head.

Colin tries to push his fur back down. The drawing looks like the web his friend Sammy Spider had built after he had bitten that teenager at a Rave party. He slowly reaches up and takes the gumleaf out of his mouth and slips it back into the packet.

Lynda looks around the room and points to Graham. "What was your name?" she asks.

"Graham."

"Before we move on, we'll do a quick recap. Or a mini-retro as I'm sure you all know we call it." She raises her hand and taps the board. "Gary, can I get you to talk us all through your understanding?"

Graham leans forward and strokes his chin. "It's *Graham*," he begins slowly. "And if I'm reading this correctly," he continues, carefully scanning the board. "We need to find *Person A*, and then *use a story*, to cause them to *sprint...*"

George leans forward and in his best Keanu Reeves - Bill and Ted voice says. "And then we will have a most Epic plan..."

Lynda looks from George to Graham, then back to George.

"Party on dude," he finishes and smiles broadly.

Bob closes his eyes and shakes his head minutely. "I can't even tell if they're doing this on purpose anymore," he mutters to himself.

"I don't see how this is relevant to me." Brenda jumps up as though she's been tazed.

"Here we go." Graham rolls his eyes.

"I don't have time for this. I've already got too much to do," Brenda ploughs on, despite the fact that no-one is paying attention. "I don't even have time for my own work, let alone telling people stories." She folds her arms tightly and glares between Bob and Lynda. "Do you even know how many people have birthdays this month?" She glares accusingly.

"Uh..." Lynda turns to Bob, who shrugs back.

"Of course you don't," Brenda huffs and looks around the room for support. "Even though the rest of them aren't as busy as me, I'm sure they've probably got better things to do as well."

Vanessa nudges Pooja and silently mouths - 'The rest of them,' in mock outrage.

"Interesting," Lynda says. "If you feel overwhelmed, then we may have an opportunity to pivot to help you."

Graham swivels left, then right, then left again. "I don't think I'm doing it right," he says raising his hand. "I still feel overwhelmed." He blinks. "And dizzy."

Lynda considers responding for a moment, then decides instead to pick up the brown marker and write - Clear the Backlog – on the board.

Colin winces. He remembers the time his mother had warned him not to eat too much cheese, but he had anyway... and had needed a special drink to help clear *his* backlog.

"Sorry," Bob interrupts Colin's thoughts. "But we're running low on time because of the mess up with the room booking," he says, holding up his watch. "Perhaps you could work through a practical example. This team has a reputation of a 'bias for action', so it might be easier for them to apply it to a real-life scenario."

Lynda scans the room. She sees Colin sitting up in his chair expectantly. Next to him Gina is pounding out what appears to be an angry text message. George, Alfred and Vanessa are trying to ignore Brenda's play for sympathy as she grumbles loudly about the cost of balloons, and silently points at her watch before throwing her hands up in frustration again.

Lynda looks back to Bob. "I'm not sure 'bias for action' is the term that immediately springs to mind," she says.

"They can be very dynamic when they need to," Bob counters, feeling slightly insulted.

"This one is asleep!" Lynda jabs her finger at Bill.

"Trust me," Graham laughs. "That actually makes this meeting much more dynamic."

Lynda rubs her eyes and takes a breath. "Okay, you can do this," she mutters to herself and silently counts to five. She looks up and waits for her eyes to come back into focus. "A practical example. How about we use *your* job as an example Gary?" she says to Graham.

Graham shifts awkwardly and makes a face that looks like he's having an attack of heartburn. He mumbles a few sentences about context and complexity, and suggests picking on Brenda's job instead.

"I've worked in multifaceted Agile operations across a broad range of industries and organisations," Lynda says confidently. "I'm sure I'll be able to follow. Now what is it you do here?"

Colin tries not to giggle when everyone spins to look at Graham at the same time. Brenda grins the way a dropbear would, just before pouncing on an unsuspecting victim. Gina leans forward on the table. "Yes Gary." She rests her chin on her hands and smiles expectantly. "What *is it* that you do here?"

Graham glares back at them, then turns to Lynda. "It's Graham," he begins. "Not Gary. And it's difficult to put into simple terms," he says.

"I'm sure I can keep up."

"Okay." Graham takes a breath and begins speaking as though he is reciting a well-rehearsed monologue in a play. "It's an amalgamation of functional and non-functional processes, combined with a series of inter-related and supplementary components, that intertwine..." He links his fingers together to demonstrate. "In a complex interplay between customers, suppliers and the business."

Lynda blinks a few times.

Vanessa whispers to George. "I'm surprised he didn't go with - It's a riddle, wrapped in a mystery, inside an enigma," she laughs.

"Let's begin by focusing on the first step, and then continue forward," Lynda says, rolling her shoulders to relieve the tension she can feel building in her neck.

Graham shrugs. "Sure. The first thing I do is create the customer requirements. That's the core foundation that the entire plan is built on."

"Okay," Lynda sighs with relief, and turns to the white board. "That's exactly what I'm looking for." She rubs a small part of the board clean and writes 'Stakeholders' in blue marker. She examines it, frowns, then rubs it out and re-writes it in green.

"What do the colours mean?" Colin asks, raising his paw.

"You don't need to raise your... Green is a more action-oriented colour." Lynda lifts the marker to the board. "The first place for us to start is to document who your stakeholders for the customer requirements are." She touches the marker to the board. "And the first would be..." she waits, pen poised to capture his response.

Colin swings his legs in time with the tick-tock of the clock in the silence.

Graham looks around. "Who's she talking to?"

"Yes, I'm speaking to you, Gary" Lynda says, looking at Graham.

He looks around and points to his chest. "Do you mean *me*?"

"Yes." Lynda attempts a confident smile, and retakes her position facing the board. She waits, pen poised for a few moments more. "Any time you're ready," she forces out, and lets her forehead drop forward lightly against the board.

"What was the question again?"

Lynda rolls her shoulders twice. "I asked - Who are your stakeholders?" She looks over her shoulder at Graham. "The people you engage with... speak to, contact? The ones who tell you what they need as part of your requirements planning." She turns back to the board and positions the pen again.

Colin hears the sound of a siren in the distance as Lynda waits.

"Sorry. Not following," Graham says flatly.

Lynda's hand drops and she spins around. "Okay. Perhaps *I'm* not making myself clear." She places her right hand against her chest, leaving a green spot from the marker on her shirt. "Even though this was covered extensively in the online training modules." She glances accusingly at Bob again. "To develop your plan, you obviously need to engage others to help determine your eventual outcomes. We call these people Stakeholders. Now in your case Gary—"

"Graham."

"As part of determining customer requirements, I would imagine that *your* Stakeholders provide you information such as customer feedback about what they like and don't like; their experience with the products; what features they would like see added or removed." She raises the corner of her mouth in what could potentially pass for another attempted smile at Graham. "So, the obvious Stakeholders for your customer requirements *would be...*" She raises her eyebrows and waits.

Graham sits back and scratches his chin thoughtfully.

Undaunted, Lynda applies the time-tested technique to increase understanding, and repeats the same sentence as before, but slower and louder. "The obvious stakeholder for your customer requirements would be *your...*" She turns back to the whiteboard ready to write.

Colin hears a car blow it's horn at someone in the car park.

Lynda takes a breath and writes *Customers* on the board. "A key stakeholder for determining customer requirements is obviously your customers." She turns and smiles broadly.

Graham rubs his chin again. "Yeah," he says. "I suppose they could be."

Lynda stares blankly and blinks. "What do you mean, you *suppose* they could be?" She scratches her head, leaving a small green spot on her forehead to match the one on her shirt. "How else could you know what the customer wants, if you don't *ask the customer?*"

Graham leans back in the chair and clasps his hands together behind his head. "I've been doing this job for twenty years," he laughs. "I think I know what the customer wants."

Bob leaps up from his chair so quickly he feels lightheaded. "Whoa..." He wobbles for a moment and grabs the table until it passes. "Are you seriously saying that every year *you* simply sit at your desk and *make up* the customer requirements?" He stares in a combination of horror and disbelief, but mainly concern about what will happen if Lynda reports this back to Andre the Giant.

"I don't see what the problem is," Graham replies, confused by all the fuss.

Bob leans forward and studies him. "When the last time was that you actually spoke to a customer?"

Graham whistles and thinks for a moment. "Spoke to one a couple of weeks ago at a BBQ," he says.

Lynda looks between Bob and Graham. "But surely you would be analysing customer feedback, sales results, trends?"

Graham scratches his head again.

"How often do you speak with the Data Analytics and Reporting Team?" Lynda asks, against her better judgement.

"Hasn't ever really come up..."

"Right," Bob says, trying to pull himself back together to quickly come up with a plan that will allow him to control the narrative. "I'll let Andre the Giant know that our Agile planning is underway, and that Graham will be speaking with the reporting team for specific customer information, and—"

"I have this room booked." A man in a dark grey suit interrupts, walking in through the open door.

Bob checks his watch. "We'll be finished in a couple of minutes Brad," he says dismissively. "Now, Let's thank Lin... Lyn—"

Brad sits down in the empty chair next to Vanessa. "I have this room booked," he repeats matter-of-factly, and begins dialling into an online meeting.

"But we'll only be another—" Bob starts to say.

Brad puts his finger to his mouth and says, "Shhh," and slides his headphones over his ears.

Lynda looks around. "Can we get another room to finish this off?"

"Sorry." Bob shrugs. "I have a clash now that I can't change," he says, calculating the time to and from the donut shop. "If Colin is prepared to give up his spot in next week's meeting, I can schedule you in." He turns and glares at Graham. "Graham should have the information from the Data team by then, so you can finish your example. If that's okay with you Colin?"

Colin nods. "Sure," he says. "I'm always happy to be flexible. Thank you for such an interesting session today Lynda. It was great!"

"With a y," Bob says quickly and smiles at Lynda.

"He was correct," Lynda says. "I'll report back to Andre the Giant about how today's meeting went, and I'll let him know that you're making the data analysis your number one priority."

Bob turns to Graham. "Did you hear that?" He declares loudly in an attempt to show Lynda how seriously he is taking it. "You need to make this your number one priority."

"If you say so, but I'm telling you, it's a waste of time," Graham protests. "They're not going to tell me anything I don't already know. I speak to Rick in Sales and Pallavi in Research and Development all the time."

"Having a beer with someone isn't considered detailed research." Bob folds his arms. "Talk to the data team."

"Fine," Graham shrugs. "I'll get on to it."

"Good." Bob says sternly and holds up his index finger. "Remember. Number one priority." He turns to Lynda. "Tell Andre we're onto it."

"Do you mind! I'm trying to have a meeting!" Brad snaps at Bob. "I've got this room booked."

Bob stares at him. "Knob," he mumbles under his breath. "Alright team," he yells and claps his hands. "Let's give Lynda a round of applause," he says loudly, staring at Brad.

"Great meeting Boss," Colin says as they leave. "Very decisive."

"Thank you Colin," Bob agrees, always happy to take praise for a job well done, even when it isn't. "And I appreciate you giving up your spot in next week's meeting. What was it you were going to present on again?"

"I was going to talk about how we can protect the environment," Colin says. "But it will be good to know more about how to apply Agile, with a capital A, to Graham's planning process." He looks over at Graham. "Especially as it's his number one priority."

"You betcha," Graham says. "Coffee?" He holds up his plastic re-usable coffee cup that reads – Plan Ahea - .

"I don't see why Bob's all heated up about the reporting thing," Graham complains, pressing the Down button for the lift. "It's just a business plan. It's not Rocket Surgery. All it's going to do is add another chunk of work that won't make any difference," he says, pushing the button again.

"You never know," Colin says. "Maybe you'll pick up something new."

"Doubtful," Graham looks up at the floor indicator and presses the button again. "If there's one thing I've learnt, my fuzzy buddy, is that the less information you have, the better."

"That seems a little... um..." Colin searches for a nice way to wrong, and settles for, "Counter-intuitive."

Graham shakes his head. "More data just invites more questions from people with no idea about what you do. Trust me. No good ever comes from having *more* data. Besides, it's impossible to get hold of anyone from the Data team to talk to." He shrugs. "I don't even know who they are."

"Oh," Colin says. "I can help you with that. I know Allanah. She works in the Data Analysis Reporting Team. Hey look," he says, pointing excitedly. "There's she is now." He waves.

Allanah sees Colin and places her cup of tea precariously on the laptop in her arms and waves back. Her hair looks like she has just fallen out of bed.

"She's the one I was just telling you about," Colin looks up at Graham. "That's a co-incidence."

"Hi Colin," Allanah walks over. "Long time no see."

"Hi Allanah," Colin says. "This is my friend Graham."

"Hey Al," Graham lifts his hand lazily in a small wave. "Good to meet you."

"Allanah," Colin whispers to him, knowing that she doesn't like to have her name shortened.

Allanah glares at him. "Hi... Gr," Allanah says, shortening Graham's name back.

"Oh right, uh, *Grr* to you too Al," Graham replies, assuming the people in data analysis growl at each other to say hello.

"Graham needs some data analysis and reporting for his yearly plan," Colin says. "Is that something your team could maybe help with? It's his number one priority."

Allanah looks down at her laptop and types quickly. Her tea sloshes unsteadily on the keyboard. "No," she says firmly. "Absolutely not."

"Oh," Colin steps back and looks up in surprise. "I... Uh..."

"Well, we tried." Graham shrugs. "Can't do more than that." He leans forward and stabs the Down button five times in rapid succession.

Allanah twitches her left arm, and the phone that was jammed between her ear and shoulder drops out of the tussle of hair, and lands neatly into her hand. "Sorry, someone asking for something that isn't in our Service Catalogue." She smiles at Colin. "What were you saying?"

Colin explains the information Graham needs in his report, and smiles hopefully.

"Okay," Allanah says, tapping a couple of keys again. "Let me just check if that's in our new Service Catalogue." Her tea sloshes over the brim of her cup and dribbles onto the keyboard.

"Maybe I'll hang onto that for you." Colin quickly reaches forward and grabs the cup before any more can overflow. "What's a Service Catalogue?"

Allanah explains that the team is trialling a new system. A comprehensive list of the services that the Data Analytics and Reporting Team offer. She tells them that having a Service Catalogue should reduce the amount of time they waste dealing with requests that fall outside of the team's scope.

"Oh, that's good then." Graham smiles. "Because what I need isn't complicated." He squints up at the lift floor indicator again and pushes the Down button a few more times. "I just need a report of last year's customer feedback," he says as the lift finally arrives with a ding. "Can I get it tomorrow?"

"You need it by tomorrow?" Allanah looks back at him in shock.

Colin nods. "Priority numero uno." He raises one claw.

Allanah shakes her head. "It's far more complex than that." She snaps her laptop shut and folds her arms around it protectively.

"Sure," Graham says and moves to one side to allow a short man in a bow tie and bowler hat to step out of the lift. "Of course." He holds his arm against the door to hold it open for Allanah and Colin. "What do I need to do?"

"You need to raise a request on our DART Board," Allanah says.

"Dart Board?" Colin furrows his brow and mimes throwing a dart. "That must take some practice to be able to request the right report."

Allanah laughs. "No, it's what we call our request page: The Data Analytics Reporting Team - Board." She lifts her head and smiles proudly. "The name was my idea."

"Clever." Colin nods.

Graham moves his shoulder to ease the slight ache from holding the lift door open. "Yeah, I just need the customer feedback. You know, complaints, that sort of thing." He switches arms.

Allanah opens her laptop again and taps a few keys. "Just select 'Bespoke Reporting' and we'll confirm it against our Service Catalogue offerings, and if it's in our scope, we'll be in touch."

"Okay, thanks." Graham swaps arms again and makes a sweeping motion into the lift. "After you," he says clearly.

Allanah looks at him blankly. "I'm not going in the lift," she says.

"Oh. After you then Colin." Graham waves him through.

"Thanks." Colin hands Allanah her tea. He steps past Graham and jumps, startled by a tall, gaunt man standing at the back of the lift. "Sorry, I didn't know you were in here..." He squints at the name on the man's security pass. "Tom." He smiles. "I'm Colin."

"Hi," Tom says quietly, rocking slightly from side to side on the spot.

"It's just down the corridor to the left." Graham points.

"Oh. Thank you, no," Tom says and checks his watch as the doors begin beeping to warn they are closing. "I'm just almost late for an important meeting."

Graham drops his arm and steps inside. "I'll throw a dart," he calls through the closing gap, rubbing his shoulder. "Or whatever you call it."

"I'll keep an eye out," Allanah calls back to him. "You should have something within four to six weeks."

Graham jabs his finger onto the Open-Door button. "Six weeks?" he gasps as the doors slide back. "I need it for *this year's* planning, not next year's!"

"Uh. Sorry," Tom says quietly, holding up his watch. "I've got a meeting to get to?"

"I'd like to help," Alannah replies. "But I'm afraid I'm bound by our Service Catalogue." She crosses her wrists together and tries unsuccessfully to pull them apart as though they're tied together.

"But didn't you just say, you're only trialling the Service Catalogue?" Graham calls back as the doors beep and begin to slide closed again.

"Yes," Allanah says, craning her head through decreasing gap.

Graham lifts his thumb off the button. The beeping stops, and he presses it again. The doors slide back open. "Then can't you just re-write it to add that *spoke reports* are something you do quickly?"

"*Be*-spoke," Allanah corrects him as the doors begin to beep again more insistently. "And no. That would defeat the entire purpose of a Service Catalogue," she says loudly over the robotic voice warning that the doors are closing. "I'll keep an eye out for your request!" she calls as the doors finally close with a clunk.

Graham shakes his head. "This place goes from worse to worst."

Colin scratches behind his ear and decides now is probably not the right time to mention that's not quite the expression.

Graham turns to Tom. "I don't know if you're any kind of expert in data analysationing..."

"Um, does he mean analysis?" Tom glances at Colin.

"Probably." Colin shrugs back and smiles.

"But I would have thought," Graham continues. "That a Data Analysis and Reporting Team's Service Catalogue would basically consist of two items, wouldn't it?" He pauses.

"Uh..." Tom raises his hands to show he has no idea. "I really couldn't say," he says reluctantly.

"One." Graham counts – one - on his index finger. "Data Analysis. And two." He counts a second finger. "Reporting. They're the Data Analysis Reporting Team," Graham continues, on a roll. "It seems to me that the activities of the team are implied in the name. They're not the - We're Just Minding This Data For Someone - Team. Or the – We Have All This Data But We Don't Really Do Anything With It - Team."

"I'm not really qualified to..." Tom holds his arms wider to appear more apologetic.

Inwardly Colin agrees that would seem to make sense, but doesn't feel it would be polite to take sides. "That would also make them WJMTDFS Team," he says. "Which isn't quite as catchy as DART."

"That *is* true." Tom agrees, and sighs with relief as the doors opens.

"You have an important meeting to get to," Colin says, stepping aside and holding the door for Tom. "After you."

"Oh, thank you." Tom smiles and steps out. "Good luck with your report," he calls back over his shoulder.

"Good luck with your meeting," Colin says. "Hey!" He turns to Graham. "I've got an idea. Why don't I go back up and grab my computer, and we can hit the DART Board at the coffee shop?"

"Good thinking," Graham agrees and pushes the button for 26. "Multi-tasking. Bob's got to be happy with that."

"Nice to meet you Tom." Colin waves as the doors close.

"What a nice Koala," Tom says to himself, then stops suddenly. "Wait." He glances around and sighs. "This isn't my floor..."

🐾🐾

"This was a bloody good idea Colin," Graham says. "I've never actually sat down here before." He looks around at the mismatched tables and chairs. "I still don't understand that though." He points to the upcycled barber's chair in the corner.

"Yeah," Colin says. "It's nice. But I don't know what it's got to do with coffee. Oh, hey Adrian." He waves to a man with a small boy bouncing beside him like a broken jack-in-the-box coming through the door.

"Busy, as usual," Graham says to him sarcastically.

"I ordered online," Adrian calls over to the counter. "Quadruple shot bullet coffee."

"Here you go," Skye, the purple haired waitress holds up a cup. "Ready to go." She holds it a few seconds longer waiting for him to collect it, then walks over and hands it to him.

Adrian takes it without saying thank you.

"I want some!" The boy bounces beside him. "Gimme some!"

"You just had two donuts Frankie," Adrian huffs, but leans forward and gives him a long swig anyway. "Bring your kid to work day." Adrian shakes his head at Graham and Colin. "Who's brilliant idea was that?" he says standing back up again.

"More!" Frankie makes a desperate grab for the cup, as his volume and bounces double in intensity.

Adrian wrestles it away. "Go look at that dentist chair or whatever it is over there or something." He points at the barber's chair.

Frankie takes off so fast that Colin is surprised he doesn't leave a cloud of dust, and races over to the chair. They all watch as he claws his way up onto the seat and begins enthusiastically punching the backrest.

"Careful Frankie," Adrian says wiping the lip of his cup. "Boisterous," he says to Colin.

"That's one word for it," Graham says as the Do Not Touch sign wobbles violently under Frankie's onslaught, before clattering loudly onto the concrete floor.

Frankie holds up his arms and bounces in victory.

"I don't know if you noticed there Adrian," Graham says pointing to the sign. "That sign there. The one that just fell down..." he trails off, letting Adrian pick up the gist.

"What about it?"

Graham stares at him. "It says - Don't Touch."

Adrian snorts and points his cup towards Frankie. "Uh, he's five?" he laughs. "Obviously he can't read." He shakes his head at Graham's stupidity.

"Here's your coffee Graham." Skye places his cup on the table. "Long black, but not too long."

Colin lifts himself up in the chair and strains to see if his is ready as well. "Hi Skye," Colin says. "Is mine nearly ready?"

"I'll check. What was it?" She smiles back.

Colin confirms it was the same order as usual - a cappuccino with extra chocolate.

Skye nods. "And what was the name for that?"

"Colin," Colin says carefully. "C O L I N."

"I'll check." Skye nods. "One sec."

"Thanks for helping with this request mate," Graham says, taking a sip of coffee. "It's probably not going to be that hard—"

"That's what she said," Adrian blurts out and laughs as though he's headlining at a comedy festival.

"Shouldn't you be keeping an eye on Clubber Lang over there?" Graham jerks his thumb towards the thumping in the corner.

"He's fine," Adrian snorts.

"Here we go," Colin says bringing up the DART Board on his computer. "Clever," he smiles. "The cursor is a dart."

Graham points to the first question. "What's this mean? Is this request Self-Service B I?" He looks at Colin. "Do I want Self-Service B I?" he asks. "What even is Self-service *B I*?"

"Boring Information?" Colin giggles.

"Sounds like one of those LBGT, LMNOP things," Adrian laughs and takes another sip of coffee.

Graham looks over at Frankie, who's initial caffeine burst appears to be wearing off. "I think round one's done," Graham says. "Shouldn't you be going over to talk to the kid's corner man?"

Colin smiles. "I'm pretty sure B I stands for Business Intelligence."

Graham huffs. "Maybe they should have been - Business Intelligent - enough to put an explanation on their so-called 'portal' then."

Colin isn't sure why Graham has chosen to place air quotes around 'portal', but lets it go. He turns to Adrian. "Oh, and it's LGBTQI," he says helpfully and smiles.

"Whatever," Adrian shrugs. "C'mon Frankie, we need to go!" he yells across the café.

"I've got a cappuccino with extra chocolate," Skye appears again holding a - Save the Environment - cup.

"Thanks." Colin smiles and holds out his paw to take it.

"It's not yours though." She shows him the name on the docket. "This one belongs to Corbin." She looks around the Café.

"I think that's mine," Colin says. "Colin."

Skye looks at the docket again. "Says Corbin."

"Yes," Colin says mustering up a half smile. "That's my cup though. And that's the coffee I ordered, from you about five minutes ago."

"Oh!" Skye puts her hand over her mouth. "I'm so sorry," she says. "The barista must have used the wrong cup. I'll get him to fix it." She looks around for Corbin again.

"No no. That's my cup and my order," Colin sighs.

"Oh," Skye says. "Here's you go then. Thanks Corbin."

"And *now* what?" Graham cries, slapping his hand on the table next to the computer. "What does *this* question mean?"

"It means you're a poo-poo head!" Frankie appears from nowhere and slams the lid shut.

"He's such a comedian!" Adrian gasps and nearly doubles over laughing.

"Hilarious," Graham says flatly, and pulls the computer to one side before Frankie can grab it.

Colin positions himself between Frankie and the laptopn. "How about we head back to the office," he says. "And you email me what you want your report to say, and I'll finish this off for you before I go home."

"Good idea," Graham scowls at Adrian and pushes his chair back.

"Always happy to help out a friend," Colin says.

"Help a poo-poo head!" Frankie yells and cackles maniacally as though he has just set off a nuclear reaction that's going to destroy the world.

"Chip off the old block," Adrian laughs proudly and ruffles Frankie's hair. "Takes after his father."

"I'm sure he does," Graham says, sliding Colin's computer under his arm. "Maybe one day you'll find out who he is."

"Morning Gina," Colin waves as she walks past on the way to her desk.

"Hey," she mumbles back, more interested in the quiz to find out which Disney Princess she would have been in a past life. "Nice jacket."

"Oh. Thanks," he says, unzipping it.

Gina takes a few more steps, then stops and turns around. "Uh... Why are you wearing a life jacket?"

"I'm helping Graham with a data analytics and reporting request," Colin says, sliding one arm out.

"O... kay." Gina frowns. "And that explains the jacket, how?"

"Oh," Colin says, pulling his other arm free and holding up the jacket to admire it. "Koalas don't really swim that well."

Gina scratches the back of her neck. "Nope. Still not seeing the connection."

"The request portal was a little complicated, so I organised a meeting with Allanah." He puts the life jacket on his desk next to his Special Reminder notebook. "Because I was going up to the Data Analysis and Business Intelligence floor, I wanted to make sure I was fully prepared. Someone told me they have a Data Lake." Colin spins around in the chair to face her, his tiny legs dangling over the seat.

"I think I'm going to need to sit down for this," Gina says, pulling over the chair from the next desk.

Colin swings his legs, a little embarrassed, causing him to slide forward on the seat. "Turns out it's not an *actual* lake," he says softly. "The entire experience wasn't what I expected at all..." his voice trails off.

"And this?" She holds up a coil of rope.

"That was for the cowboys—" Colin starts to say, but Gina stops him before he can continue.

"No. Don't tell me." She taps her finger on her lips a few times. "I want to guess." She taps again. "The... *cowboys...*" She racks her brain. "I know this place is full of cowboys, but not the type that use rope..."

"Allanah had said someone from the team would need to do some data wrangling. So—"

"Ah. Data *wrangling...* cowboys." She drops the rope back on the desk. "Got it. Easy mistake to make."

"I was really looking forward to talking to the cowboys about Rosebud McRae," Colin frowns. "I even made a point of watching the documentary that came out a few months ago again to make sure I was up to speed," he sighs softly. "This is the type of rope he uses." He says, picking it up.

Gina watches him fiddle with the ends of the rope sadly. "Yeah." She reaches over and pats his paw. "I guess that kinda sucks. I know he's one of the cowboys you've mentioned before."

Colin nods up at her. "He's my favourite," he says glumly.

"Did you at least get the answers you needed?" Gina asks, feeling bad for him and trying to change the subject.

"Yeah, I did." He nods slowly, and pauses. "Wait," he says, a look of realisation lights up his face.

"Um. Are you okay?" Gina says leaning forward on the chair. "Do I need to call First Aid?"

"I'm better than okay." Colin's smile widens. "I was feeling a little down because of this whole misunderstanding thing, but you just helped me realise that even though I didn't get to talk about Rosebud McRae, or go kayaking, I still found the answers I needed, helped my pal Graham get the information he wanted..." He beams. "And, I learned about how data analysis and reporting work, so next time I'll be able to help even quicker." He rubs his chin thoughtfully. "Maybe I can even talk to Bob about being our DART Boat Champion!" He sits back.

"Sure," Gina says. "I'll order you a pint glass."

"And..." Colin bounces on his chair. "I finally got around to re-watching the Rosebud McRae documentary that I'd been too busy to find time for."

Gina shakes her head lightly in disbelief. "I dunno how you stay so upbeat," she says pushing her chair back. One of the wheels catches on a snag in the carpet, and it stops suddenly, causing her to bang her leg. "Most days I want to stab half the people here before lunch."

Colin laughs. "Surely that's not true."

Gina frowns. "No, you're right." She turns toward her desk. "It doesn't usually take until lunch." She pulls out her phone again and starts limping away. "Wait." She notices something from the corner of her eye. "What's *that* for?" She points under his desk.

"Oh. That was for the data mining," Colin says holding up a long white fake beard and a shovel. "I'm already small, so this was to help fit in with the other data-miners. It's not often I get to work with others my own height."

Gina blinks twice. "Is that a Snow-White reference?" she says.

"Turns out it's just a term for finding for data patterns." Colin shrugs. "I might keep this in case I get invited to a fancy dress party." He drops it back under the desk. "I'm not sure what to do with this pick-axe though..."

"Any word yet from Allanah's team?" Colin asks walking up to Graham's desk.

"Ha!" Graham laughs and takes a sip of coffee from his plastic re-usable coffee cup that reads – 'I'm a mushroom, they keep me in the dark and feed me on bullshit' – and puts it on his desk next to a stack of paper, almost as tall as the cup. "Any word?" He picks the paper up with both hands and holds it up in front of him. "Plenty of words."

"What's that?" Colin asks.

"It's the bloody report," Graham snorts.

"Gosh. No wonder it takes them so long to create it," Colin gasps. "It's huge."

"Huge alright," Graham laughs derisively. "Huge waste of time." He drops the pile back on the desk with a thump. "It's pointless."

"Pointless?" Colin looks up at him. His heart speeds up. "I hope I didn't make a mistake." He chews on his nail. "It took me a long time to fill in the portal request. And then I spent an hour alone just finding the right rope."

"Rope?"

"For the cowboys— never mind. What's wrong with it?" He reaches forward and straightens the pile.

Graham waves that it is okay to leave it crooked. "No. You did a great job little buddy, thanks. But it turns out the file was too big to email. And they couldn't put it on a USB because USBs are blocked. So until they get it sorted, this is their workaround." He slaps his hand on top of the pile. "Hard copy."

"Oh," Colin stares at the stack. "That seems like far too much information to go through on paper."

"It is," Graham says, picking it up again." It's full of design data, contract information, financial stuff. And the only bit *I* need..." He hefts the paper from one arm to the other sorting through to near the middle. A few pages to flutter onto the floor. "Is this." He whips out a page with a flourish, causing some more pages to slide out and float downwards. The pile in his left arm tilts and threatens to slide loose.

"Maybe you should put it back on the desk," Colin says.

Graham drops the pile down and holds out five pages. "The main information I was after, was in this section."

Colin reaches forward and takes them. "This looks like my nose," he says looking at a page with a solid black circle in the middle of the page, and touches his nose.

"Not a nose," Graham says. "It's a pie chart."

Colin squints and holds the page up to the light. "A pie chart?"

"Yep. A pie chart of types of customer feedback and complaints by demographics. But, because our printers only print black and white now..." He holds up three more pages with solid black circles. "Every pie chart looks like this." He flicks to the next page, which has six more black circles. "This is the sales breakdown by region," he snorts. "Or maybe one side of a dice. And, oh yeah, don't let me forget..." He ruffles through the pile. "Wait till you see the annual costs by expenses, operating costs, margins and gross profit. Organised by region and segment."

"Isn't that exactly what we asked for?" Colin asks.

"Yep," Graham says and holds out two more pages.

Colin takes them, turns one sideways... Then upside down. "It looks like a silhouette of the city at night?" He squints and extends his arm as far as he can to hold the paper further away.

"No, my fuzzy buddy," Graham laughs. "That; is seven, count them, seven, stacked column charts, showing the breakdown of expenses. Instead of giving me a table of figures, they put together this abomination of ink and stupidity."

"That doesn't seem very helpful," Colin says sliding the pages back into the middle of the report. "When will you get it electronically?"

Graham shrugs. "They told me to call the Help Desk and see if they could work something out."

"Hopefully that won't be necessary." Colin shudders involuntarily. "But don't you need it for the next planning meeting with Lynda?"

Graham stands up. "Bob said Andre the Giant told him he'd lost interest and was onto some other new thing now, so Lynda has been moved onto that."

"Is that actually what he said?" Colin asks in surprise.

"Reading between the lines," Graham answers. "Which I won't be doing with this thing." He pushes the stack of paper in disgust.

"Can you use any of it for your plan?"

"Oh, my plan's submitted already," Graham says.

Colin scratches behind his ear. "I'm confused. If you *needed* the figures in the report to create your plan, but you couldn't use them, where did they come from?"

"Made 'em up of course."

POP! goes the tuft of fur on the top of Colin's head.

"You.... made them up?"

"Sure," Graham says. "Bob said it was my number one priority, remember. So I did the same as I do every year. Take last year's plan, add 20% to the costs, change the colours, see what notes I made from Rick and Pallavi at the Christmas party, and then drop in any development updates I know are coming up."

"But what will you say when he asks if you talked to the analytics team and got the data?" Colin says, concerned.

Graham laughs. "I'll tell him the truth." He picks up the report again. "I spoke to Allanah, we filled out the request thing and they sent me the report. He doesn't need any more details than that. And I don't need all that mumbo jumbo we've had about being Agile and talking to Snakeherders—"

"Stakeholders," Colin corrects him helpfully.

"Stakeholders, snake charmers, space heaters, whatever," Graham replies. "Told you it was a waste of time. Just added all that extra effort for nothing," he says. "Anyway, plan's done. Mission Accomplished. Time for coffee I reckon." He glares at the report, spreading across his desk. "I'll get rid of this testament to insanity on the way." He snatches at the jumbled stack of paper. Two pages titled 'Confidential Pricing' float casually to the floor.

"I'll grab those," Colin says, picking them up.

Graham twists around. "Thanks mate," he says over his shoulder, causing four more pages to slip out.

Colin picks them up on his way too, and stuffs them into the slot on the almost overflowing secure bin in the utility room. "That was lucky. Just enough room," he says to himself and catches up to Graham. "Only just enough room in the secure—" Colin says as he steps around the corner into the kitchen and sees Graham leaning all his weight forward to force his stack of paper into the rubbish bin. "Uh. I don't think a report with sales figures and next year's plans should go in the kitchen bin." Colin frowns.

Graham stands back and brushes his hands together. "Secure one's full," he says. "Anyway, a bin's a bin, it all ends up in the same place."

"I'm not sure it does." Colin looks back towards the utility room.

"Besides, it takes too long. Those tiny slots in the lid." Graham mimes sliding paper into the slot and yawns. "You can only do a few sheets at a time." He leans over and gives the bin one final push down. "That'll be okay," he says rinsing his hands under the tap. "Coffee time."

"Okey dokey. I'll meet you at the lift," Colin says, scooting out the door and almost bumping into Bob. "Hi Boss." He looks at his watch. "Late lunch?" "You know how it is," Bob sighs. "Oh. If you see Graham, can you remind him he needs to submit his plan."

"I thought he said he did that last week," Colin says. "But I'll check. Enjoy your lunch boss." Colin waves and turns towards the lift. Behind him he hears a commotion, and pokes his head back around the corner.

"Graham!" Bob yells, waving a fistful of paper angrily. "Is this report yours?" He shakes it again. A withered slice of pickle flicks off and lands on his cheek. "Ow, yuck! Jesus!" He disappears back into the kitchen and splashes his face with water.

"Dunno what his problem is, his precious plan is done," Graham says pressing the Down button for the lift. "And I put it most of it in the recycling."

A company is only as good as its ~~people~~ KOALA

"Final item before we close the meeting out." Bob turns to point at the agenda on the screen behind him, revealing the large sweat patch under his arm.

Graham shifts in his chair and pulls his collar away from his neck. "Is it getting the bloody air conditioning fixed in this room?"

"Did you put in a repair request on the intranet like I told you to?" Bob turns slowly and raising his eyebrows.

There's a few seconds of silence before Graham leans back in his chair casually. "Not my job."

"Then you've forfeited your right to complain," Bob replies smugly and turns back to the screen.

"Bet he hasn't," Brenda snorts.

Bob ignores her and points back at the screen. He holds his hand as steady as he can, his finger aimed accusingly at the final item on the agenda. "HR informs me that no-one has accepted the invite for the workshops to go through the 'How you doin'' survey results..." He glares around the table at each of them. He doesn't add that his manager Andre chewed him out for lack of participation, and to save himself, he had volunteered his team to take part. He feels a twinge in his tricep, but continues to point. "It's not that I'm angry," he says, his tone becoming more sombre. "I'm disappointed."

Gina's gaze moves thoughtfully up from her phone, to focus on Bob. "I can live with that," she says and goes back to her quiz to identify whether she would have survived the bubonic plague.

"I accepted them Boss!" Colin calls, raising his paw.

Vanessa takes a sip of her coffee and shrugs. "Yeah. Can't. In the middle of something." She thinks for a second. "Budget meeting."

"I'm pleased that our organisation cares enough to listen." Umi smiles. "But unfortunately it clashes with my project meeting update."

Pooja shrugs apologetically. "And I'm making an important phone call at that time."

Bob shifts his gaze to her. "With who?" he asks.

"Um," Pooja shifts uncomfortably in her chair and looks around. "George!" She points at him triumphantly.

"Oh yeah," George shrugs. "I can't make it either."

"If you're just talking to each other." Bob looks between them. "Can't you reschedule?"

"It was the only space we could find." They both reply in unison. In perfect timing they look at each other, then at Bob, then back to each other and shrug, as though it's out of their hands.

"I'm with you Boss!" Colin jumps in again excitedly. "I love workshops. I even moved my monthly meeting with Margaret from Marketing and flicked my fortnightly with Frank from Finance so I could be there."

"Thanks Colin," Bob mumbles and turns to Graham. "And what about you Graham? What

71

'meeting clash' do you have that will mean you can't make it?"

"No meeting," Graham shakes his head slightly, without looking up from his phone. "Just not interested."

Bob squeezes his eyes closed for a moment. "For god's sake Graham. You can't say that," Bob sighs. "Are you even listening? Is there something more important on your phone than what's happening here?"

Graham jerks his head up. "Oh. Yes. Sorry. You're right. I wasn't giving you my undivided attention. I didn't mean to say - I'm not interested." He holds up his hands apologetically.

"Thank you."

"I *meant* to say - I don't care. It's pointless." Graham folds his arms tightly. "Nothing's going to change. I've been telling them about the same problems for years."

"It seems like you're good at *identifying* the problem, Graham. But not good at *fixing* the problem," Bob says, resisting the temptation to mime a mic drop. "I've never seen you at any of the improvement workshops, or volunteering to provide detailed feedback on any of these so-called issues." Bob adds smugly. "All you do is point to what's wrong."

"I can't be expected to do everything."

Colin pushes himself higher in the chair. "I think it will be great to be part of a meeting run by Human Resources boss," he calls out again, a little louder. "They must be so professional and slick to be doing that job."

"Thanks Colin," Bob says. He lifts his hand to point at the others. He feels a cramp in the muscle on the back of his hand. "I need to go see Allanah from Analytics and Reporting now, so we'll pick this up later." He snatches up his computer. "I'll be expecting to see you all at the HR meeting."

"I'll be there..." Colin's voice trails off as Bob storms out of the room and slams the door.

George looks around to the others. "So, we're done here then?"

"After you little buddy," Graham says as they join the meandering line, inching their way along the corridor towards the big meeting room.

"Thanks," Colin says and ducks to avoid a backpack as the person in front of him turns. "I'm glad Bob reminded everyone to re-check their schedules to be able to make it to the meeting."

"If by re-check, you mean - pestered incessantly," Graham snorts.

Colin shuffles a few more steps forward with the queue as it moves towards the room. "I think it will be helpful to learn about our strengths and opportunities," he says.

"Opportunities to make us work harder," Graham nudges the man with the backpack and laughs. "Am I right?" He nudges him with his elbow again to drive the point home.

"Can you not do that please?" The man turns, causing Colin to duck again.

"Sorry mate." Graham holds his hands up innocently. "I thought you were someone else. I was just saying though that these things are all about how

HR can help the company screw us over." He taps him on the shoulder again.

"If you have concerns about the results," he sniffs haughtily. "Contact the HR CARE-Line for support."

Colin weaves his head sideways like a boxer slipping a jab as the man turns to point to the poster on the wall. The image shows four people on the phone to the CARE-Line. Three appear concerned, while the fourth smiles as though they know something the others don't. A woman wearing an old-style telephone operator headset dominates the image, leaning back with a broad grin to show how happy she is to be able to help the callers. Underneath in thick dark font the tag-line reads: Have concerns about your work? - Tell it to someone who cares.

Colin scratches behind his ear as they trudge past it. Before he can mention that there's no phone number, the plain grey wall becomes glass, and he gasps, peering into the Big Meeting Room. "Gosh!" he says, pushing his nose against the window. "This room is bigger than my house." He wipes the smudge off and points to a huge colour poster that says:

There is no **I** in **T E A M!**

"That's good spelling," he says to himself. It reminds him Mrs Wombat's class, when she would write the words on the board so everyone knew how to spell them. The procession continues slowly forward the way condemned prisoners do, until it finally spills through the door like the overflow of a dam.

Colin stops and takes in the huge space. The walls are covered in posters that read: 'Team Work makes the Dream Work' and 'We Win When We Work Well... Together!'

"Over here buddy," Graham calls and Colin scoots across to the chairs in the back row.

"Look!" Colin points excitedly. "That whole wall is a giant whiteboard! And there's a drawing corner too." He gawks at a series of different coloured boxes, lines and circles. Some have arrows joining them together, others are crossed out. He tilts his head this way and that. He can't work out what it's a picture of, but he can tell that whoever drew it had had lots of fun.

His eyes follow a long arrow to where someone had been practicing maths. Whoever it was had unsuccessfully tried to rub out a column of numbers with dollar signs, and a graph with a red arrow pointing straight down. Next to the graph; where somebody has tried to scribble over the word 'Profit', there is a piece of paper stuck to the wall with: 'This part of the wall is not a whiteboard! Do not write here!' in big red letters.

"Hey look," Colin nudges Graham. "It's Arthur. He brought me my forms to fill in and welcomed me on my first day. Hi Arthur!" He waves.

"If everyone can sit down please," Arthur calls out impatiently, even though more than half the group are still trying to make their way into the room. He presses the remote control to switch on the two huge TV screens behind him. They flash once and begin to fade in slowly.

"Great seats," Colin says settling in. "Good choice Graham."

A tall man with a bald spot, a ponytail and a red checked shirt moves slowly along the row of empty seats drops into the chair directly in front of Colin.

"Now I can't see." Colin strains to look past the bald head in front of him. He stands on his tip-toes, then gives up, and climbs up on the chair.

"No standing on the furniture please," Sally from Safety calls over curtly.

Colin frowns and climbs down. "I think there might be a spot down the front," he says to Graham. "I'll check if there's a spare for you too," he calls back over his shoulder and squeezes past the remaining people coming in.

"If everyone could settle down and take a seat please." Arthur repeats more loudly than before, even though there are still people in the corridor.

"Wow, look at these seats!" Colin stares at the four empty rows at the front. He spins around and waves to Graham. "There's still a couple left!" he calls out, and scoots across to the middle of the front row. "I hope they're not reserved for special guests or VIPs," he says quietly, looking around for anyone who might look important.

"Let's get this thing started," Arthur addresses the room again, then immediately turns his back to the audience and begins fiddling with his computer. He presses a few keys, and one of the TV screens begins to fill with people.

Colin knows that they are on screen because they are 'virtually working'. He's not sure exactly what that means, because Bob often says the same thing about Graham, and he's always in the office.

"Can I squeeze in?" Graham drops onto the seat beside Colin.

"Hey." Colin smiles and taps him on the arm. "I thought you'd stay up the back."

Graham shakes his head. "Can't leave my little buddy stuck down here on his lonesome." He smiles and leans back. The chair lets out a disconcerting crack, and he slowly leans forward again. "Besides, who else am I going to point out stuff like that to?" He nods towards the people on the screen. "Second row down, on the right. Steve from Marketing."

Colin glances over. "Second row down... Steve from... Ah!" He jumps back in the chair.

Steve's head fills half the frame with the camera looking up at him from his desk, making him look like a movie villain who's about to ask for a billion dollars or he'll destroy a major capital city. Towering behind him over his left shoulder is a huge painting.

"I've never seen a life size painting of a clown before," Colin breathes in slowly, waiting for his heart-rate to return to normal. "Why would anyone want something like that staring over their shoulder while they're working?" He wraps his arms slowly across his chest.

Graham shrugs. "Probably not that different to what we have with Bob if I think about it."

"Anyone sitting here?" A young man in jeans and a Minecraft T-Shirt points to the empty seat next to Colin, and sits down without waiting for an answer.

Colin holds out a paw, and introduces himself and Graham.

"I'm Mike, the Intern," Mike says.

"If I can have your attention, I'd like to get started," Arthur says without actually starting the meeting again. The second TV flickers twice, fades out and then and slowly fades in to show Arthur's presentation slides in outline mode.

Colin leans forward and peers at the collection of tiny slides on the screen. "This must be a very important meeting." Colin whistles. "Look how many slides there are!"

Arthur makes some final adjustments to the size of his slides, eventually stopping when the screen shows the first slide – 1 of 94, and the top quarter of the next one.

Colin makes a note in his Special Reminder Notebook to ask Arthur why it's better to show all the slides and the notes on the screen, rather than using presentation mode.

"Welcome to today's meeting—" Arthur begins as the final stragglers loiter for a space in the back rows.

"We don't know who you are!" Brenda calls out. "Can you at least introduce yourself?" She leans back in her chair and shakes her head in annoyance.

Arthur slowly raises his arm to show the remote clicker in his hand and stares directly at Brenda. He presses the button and the slides scroll awkwardly up the screen. It reads: 'I'm Arthur from the Human Resources Department'. Without breaking eye contact, Arthur says, "I'm Arthur, from the Human Resources Department."

"Thank you." Brenda looks around smugly, with the confidence that she had somehow influenced this introduction.

Arthur glares at her for a moment longer. "Today's meeting..." he continues.

"Can't hear you!" A disembodied voice calls from the back.

Arthur coughs once, scowls and takes a breath. "TODAY'S MEETING!" he yells, causing the first five rows of people to move their chairs backwards. "Is to discuss the results of our annual 'How You Doin' survey, and identify the key areas that you believe will improve your engagement and motivation." He presses the clicker, and the screen jerks upwards to show the top half of the next slide.

Colin wriggles on the chair in an attempt to get comfortable; but eventually gives up and just settles in the best he can while Arthur moves slowly over to the whiteboard wall. He notices that on the bottom left, someone has drawn a small dick and balls.

Arthur rubs out the complicated diagram under the heading 'Do Not Erase' and scribbles - Motivated Employees are Happy Employees! in thick black marker.

At least, that's what Colin thinks it says, because it actually looks more like - Mulvurter Emplayes are Haffj Employ~.

"I can't see what you're pointing at," says one of the virtually working people.

"It doesn't matter," Arthur responds.

"What did he say?" another voice asks.

"Don't ask me. I can't see what he's pointing at."

Arthur's shoulders slump and he steps closer to the computer microphone. "I'm not pointing at *anything*," he growls. "I'm writing on the whiteboard."

"I can't see what you're writing."

Arthur snatches his computer and types - Motivated Employees are Happy Employees! - on the slide. He grabs the mouse and jerks the cursor in haphazard strokes across the screen, before circling around the words motivation and engagement. "There," he says.

Colin tries to keep track of the cursor, but needs to stop when he feels a little dizzy and hears a warning gurgle from his stomach.

"If everyone is alright for me to move on now," Arthur says, making it clear that he's not framing it as a question. He presses 'Mute All' before they can answer, and continues making his way through the slides.

Colin listens carefully when Arthur eventually gets to the agenda on slide nine and makes a note to check if he will need a permission slip for the journey Arthur says they are all going on together.

He nudges Graham excitedly. "We must be going to a playground." He bounces on the chair when Arthur shows more slides about how they will be moving needles, shifting dials and pulling levers.

Colin gulps when Arthur says they will need to hit the ground running. He's not very fast because of his tiny legs, and doesn't want to let anyone down. He glances down and gives them a few practice swings back and forth.

When Arthur says that going forward they will need all hands on deck to co-ordinate a deep dive, Colin lifts his paw to his mouth and whispers to Graham that he might see if he can stay home that day. Because Koalas aren't really known for their swimming ability.

Arthur continues to the next section of the presentation, which explains how the survey works, the collection method, normalisation of the results, and how the colours for the graphs were determined, tested and finally agreed upon. "Here, on slide fifty-seven—"

"Is any of this relevant?" a self-important looking man asks loudly, adjusting his jacket.

"Of course it is," Arthur snaps, with no idea if it is or not. "If it wasn't, the survey company wouldn't have included it in the slide pack they provide to us with the results."

"What does - Background only, not for distribution - mean?" Mike the intern asks, pointing at the bottom of the screen.

Colin moves around on the chair again, and tries to ignore the dull ache that is beginning in his lower back, and notices a nice lady with very white teeth on one of the screens waving to him.

Colin smiles and waves back. "Hi Melissa," he mouths to her, reading her name off the screen. He watches as she opens and closes her mouth over and over again.

'Looks like she's hungry,' Colin thinks, remembering how Mrs Sparrow's babies would yell for food at meal time. He checks his watch and sees it's nearly time for lunch. "I'm feeling a bit 'peckish' myself," he giggles, and opens and closes his mouth a few times.

On the screen above the hungry bird lady, and to the left of Steve and his clown painting, Colin notices a very thin bald man with a busy red beard moving his hands rapidly up and down. "Hmm. Okay," Colin says and rubs his chin. "If I'm not mistaken, I think he saying..." he turns to Graham. "Two words. And the first word sounds like... Chicken?" He cups his hands and mouths at the screen, "Is it a book or a film?"

Arthur notices Colin and looks around to the TV. He sees several people pointing to the Microphone icon. He sighs and turns the mute function off.

"... HEAR US!" The red-bearded man's voice booms from the speaker.

"Oh, no. You're not allowed to talk in charades." Colin shakes his head. "That's cheating."

The hungry baby-bird lady grumpily crosses her arms. "Can you hear me now?" she yells. "I have a question about—"

Colin tries to listen, but he can't make out what she's saying over the noise of someone chewing, several dogs barking, a reminder alarm, one side of a phone call, a loud tappity-tapping noise, and what sounds like the climax of the movie Die Hard.

"I've turned the global mute off, so if can you put *yourself* on mute when you're not speaking, please," Arthur says and taps his foot impatiently.

Slowly the sounds begin to disappear.

"Yeah, he's an idiot. Whoops."

The chewing stops, and most of the talking goes quiet with a few snippets continuing before it finally settles down.

"Rover! For Christ's sake, will you shut the fu— sorry."

Everyone laughs when they hear, "Oh shit!" and Alan Rickman suddenly disappearing halfway through his final monologue.

"Thank you," Arthur says. "As I was saying—" he starts and is interrupted by the 'tappity-tap' noise again.

"If," Arthur says very slowly and clearly. "You. Are. Not. Talking. Can you put yourself on mute," he huffs. "*Please.*"

Colin makes a note in his Special Reminder Notebook of how Arthur gives clear instructions to ensure there's no confusion or misunderstanding, and underlines that Arthur always says please.

The room waits patiently for another twenty seconds until the 'tappity-tapping' finally stops.

"Thank you," Arthur says. "Now if I can continue?" he goes on without waiting for an answer. "Now here—"

"You didn't answer my question," the hungry baby-bird lady snaps at him.

Arthur slowly takes his glasses off and rubs his eyes. "What was your question?" he sighs.

Colin watches her open and close her mouth a few times. "I think she's on mute again," he says.

The lady stops moving her mouth. "Well, I can't remember now after all that kerfuffle." She stabs her mute button and folds her arms defiantly.

"I'm glad that's resolved then," Arthur mumbles putting his glasses back on. "Now—"

"I'm on my phone," a gruff voice bursts out from the TV. Colin tries to see who it is, but their camera is off, and they have changed their display name to - 'Alpha'. "Did we need video for this?"

"I told you, I'm in a meeting. Go ask your mother."

Colin scratches his ear and wonders why Alpha's mother would know whether he needed video or not. 'Maybe she works with Arthur,' he thinks.

"Yes, Rick." Arthur says ignoring Rick's 'Alpha' display name. "You need video. When I'm finished with the background slides. I'll be going through the results of our How You Doin' survey."

"How many more slides is that?" Rick barks in the most Alpha way as he can.

Arthur glances at his screen. "There's only eighteen more. So, if you'd like to be able to see the results, I'd suggest you log in via your computer."

"I'm driving," Rick snaps, as though it should be obvious that's everyone's default position for an online meeting. "The invite didn't say we needed video."

"The invite *did* say you needed video," Arthur snaps back.

"I don't see anywhere that it says video."

Arthur turns to the TV and puts his hands on his hips. "I thought you said you were driving?"

"No point in being here if there's no slides," Rick snorts, ignoring Arthur's line of logic.

"There *are* slides." Arthur replies, pointing at his computer.

"I can't see any."

"Because you're driving maybe?"

"Don't worry mate," Graham calls out. "There's plenty of slides, and you're not missing anything. He's read every single word on every slide."

Colin nods and smiles. It reminds him of how Mrs Wombat used to read to them off the board. "Such professionalism," he gives Arthur a thumbs up.

Arthur leans down to his computer and moves the meeting invite over the top of his presentation. "Here Rick," he says scrolling through the invite.

"Uh. He doesn't have video," Gina points out helpfully.

There's a few moments silence as Arthur scrolls rapidly. The text blurs its way up and down the screen. Colin looks closely to try and help, but his stomach grumbles again, so he closes his eyes and takes a few deep breaths. He hears in the second row dry retch.

"He's gone anyway," Mary from Marketing says, pointing to the screen where Alpha was.

Arthur ignores her, and the increasing murmurings of people swapping ways to stop motion sickness and continues to scroll the invite up and down rapidly.

Mike the Intern leans forward and squints at the scrolling screen. "Where does it say video?"

"It should be obvious you need video," Arthur snaps at him and closes the invitation, without finding anything about video. "You shouldn't need to be told that. We're a professional organisation—"

"Can we skip the background and move on," the bald man with the ponytail calls out from the back of the room.

Arthur stares at him for a moment, and checks how many of the slides have 'Not for Distribution' on them and skips ahead to the next section, titled – Results. He fiddles with the position of the slide to try and get it to sit in the centre of the screen, eventually gives up and cuts off the bottom quarter.

He turns slowly back to the room. "For some reason," he begins, pushing his glasses down his nose to look over the top of them. "Our overall engagement score dropped by 22% from last year." He glares at each person in the room as though it was a personal attack on him. "Would anyone care to provide any thoughts or insights on why that might be?" He folds his arms and waits.

Colin notices a clock softly ticking on the side wall. He notices it's forty-five minutes slow.

After a few more moments of silence, a lone voice calls out. "How far did it drop?"

"Twenty two percent," Arthur says. "Which I just told you. Do you have any thoughts on why?"

"If I had to guess," the man shrugs, "I'd probably go with incompetent management."

A murmur of agreement makes it way across the room.

"No consequences for people who don't deliver?" Comes a call from a lady near the back.

"For me, it's the rampant nepotism—"

Arthur holds up his hands for them to stop. "I doubt it is any of those things," he says flatly. "Does anyone have anything more constructive to add?"

"No work/life balance," says someone to Colin's left, kicking off a new round of suggestions.

"I'd probably vote for toxic culture."

"Nah, under-resourced because of the hiring freeze."

"Incompetent management!" calls a loud voice from over Colin's shoulder.

"I'd definitely agree with that," Graham laughs, looking behind him. "But we've had that one already Bob."

"I meant *Senior* Management," Bob corrects him. "Not that I think that," he quickly adds, scanning the room to check that there're no Senior Management present. "I was only suggesting what *others* may incorrectly believe."

"I'll be sure to pass you're concerns on," Arthur narrows his eyes at Bob, who shrinks back into the chair. "Does anyone else have anything to say?"

Sally from Safety raises her hand. "Because management keep screwing us over for our bonuses?" she offers.

"Yeah, I'd go with that one too." And another murmur of agreement flows across the room like a wave at a football game.

"Well, that's clearly *not* the case," Arthur says defensively. He crosses his arms tightly over his chest, accidentally pressing the clicker, causing the presentation behind him to advance through to the final slide. "There is no 'screwing over' as you say. Our Bonus Calculation algorithm is a simple process, designed to ensure fairness and parity."

"Can you explain it to us?" Sally asks, tilting her head slightly.

Arthur stares at her for a long moment, then says that he doesn't have time to go into the complexities of the algorithm right now, but that he's more than happy to schedule a deep dive with the General Manager of HR, if anyone feels they can't trust the company or their HR department to treat them fairly.

A few people shift uncomfortably as Arthur reorganises the slides back to the correct place. "Following extensive analysis of the results," Arthur begins, lining up a slide with a graph on it, that cuts off the bottom scale. "We have identified the key areas that appear to be causing concern for employees..." He points definitively at the screen behind him.

"I'd agree with that," Vanessa calls out, and everyone laughs.

Arthur turns, confused, to the main TV monitor which is dark and displaying - Timed Out due to lack of activity.

"There's no need for sarcasm," Arthur says and fiddles with the screen until a slide that reads – Top Areas for Improvement Opportunities. While Arthur finishes with the display, Graham lifts his hand and places it against his forehead like a fortune teller.

"Are you okay?" Colin asks, looking up at Graham, concern furrowing his brow.

"It's fuzzy," Graham says slowly, pretending to be deep in concentration. "Wait... Yes, I can see it now... I predict..." he pauses. "The opportunities will be... A lack of faith in leadership... Our systems and processes don't support us, and... No-one believes anything will change based on the results of this survey." He slumps back in the chair dramatically. "I must rest."

Colin giggles.

Arthur adjusts the slide to almost be in the middle of the frame. "The top opportunities for improvement are in the following areas," he pauses. "A lack of faith in leadership, systems and processes don't support us, and no-one believes anything will change based on the results of this survey."

Colin's mouth drops open in shock and he stares at Graham. "Wow! Are you psychic?"

Graham shakes his head. "Nah. Same every year." He folds his arms and gets comfortable again.

"This year there was one new item that stood out above all of these," Arthur continues. "And which will receive a special focus. It's…" He stops and looks around the room as though he's about to announce the winner of the Best Picture at the Oscars, and flicks to the next slide. "I spend too much time in unnecessary meetings. Whatever that means," he says in a mocking tone. "But it's not up to me to judge why that's wrong," he says, making it clear that he believes it is. "The spirit of the survey is to allow *you* to determine that for yourselves." He presses the clicker and the slides move to show the top half of – Overall results. "Now we can get into the meat of the presentation—"

He's interrupted by a loud Bing! from his computer, and a reminder for a 'pre-meeting to talk about what needs to be included in next week's prep discussion' pops up over the presentation. He sighs. "Well, it appears that due to Rick's mistake about the video, Melissa's audio difficulties, and the unruliness earlier, we're running out of time." He checks his watch. "I'll extend this session for another fifteen minutes to cover this off this slide about this new special category."

Graham slowly raises his hand. "The 'I spend too much time in unnecessary meetings' special category?" he asks.

Arthur says yes in a way that implies he believes Graham is simple, and clicks to advance to two-thirds of the next slide.

"I've got another meeting to get to," Ponytail says and stands up.

Arthur huffs and checks his watch. "We're not even at the end of the original allocated time for this meeting yet."

Ponytail shrugs and moves awkwardly past the others in the row towards the door.

Arthur continues talking and moves ponderously through the next eight slides.

"I need to go to the toilet," Vanessa stands up and heads towards the door.

"I have to go as well."

"Me too."

"Me three."

"Can't you wait?" Arthur grumbles as a procession begins to form out the door. "We'll just be another few minutes."

"You said that ten minutes ago," the third escapee replies, dancing from one foot to the other. "After we got to the end of the extra fifteen minutes, and we're still hearing about why you used a pie chart instead of a bar chart!" She presses her legs together tightly.

"It's important that everyone has appropriate context." Arthur replies, adjusting his glasses.

A man in a polo shirt nudges his neighbour and motions towards the door with his head. They mumble that they need to get to another meeting, or maybe that something that has to take priority has unexpectedly come up.

Colin watches as more and more people take the advantage of the unplanned exodus towards safety.

"Fine then," Arthur grunts as more people stand up. "I'll schedule a supplementary, follow-up session for later this week..." he pauses and melodramatically adds, " *With video.*" He adjusts his glasses. "So we can go through the remaining twenty slides we didn't cover today, thanks to *some* people who were disruptive."

"I'm sorry," Graham says raising his hand again. "Can I just confirm you're saying, that because we didn't get through everything you wanted to in this meeting; that ran over the *extended time* you added on..."

"Yes."

"That you're now going to arrange another meeting..."

"Go on."

"To catch up on the content we didn't get to today..."

"And too recap of course."

"Of course," Graham waves his hand as though it's so obvious it barely requires mentioning.

"And then we'll begin planning for the series of brainstorming sessions." Arthur closes the lid on his laptop.

"Sorry?" Graham raises his eyebrows in a combination of confusion and disbelief. "Series of brainstorming sessions?"

"Yes." Arthur nods.

"To try and identify why people think they're spending too much time in meetings."

"Yes," Arthur says matter-of-factly and takes his glasses off and wipes them on his shirt. He checks for smudges, frowns and wipes them again. "Was there anything else?"

"Nope." Graham says. "No, I think that pretty well sums it up."

"If there's no other questions." Arthur slips his glasses back on and unplugs his computer. "I'll see you all later in the week then," he says walking past several people who have their hands raised.

Bob stands in front of the team holding a yellow manila folder. He stares at them solemnly, then lifts the folder and shakes it lightly, in an obvious attempt to convey the importance of the information held within.

"Do you need a heartburn tablet boss?" Colin calls out, rummaging through his pencil case.

"No, thank you," Bob says and slaps the folder theatrically onto the meeting room table with a thwack.

Gina leans over to George. "Dramatic."

"Okay team," Bob says, still standing. "At today's meeting we're going to talk through the annual survey results."

"Didn't we almost do this yesterday with Arthur?" Vanessa says, bending over awkwardly to reach the lever to raise her chair.

"No." Bob taps the folder twice. "*These* results are specific to our team."

Colin raises his paw. "I thought the survey was anonymous?"

Bob nods and explains that the survey *is* completely anonymous. But, so HR can provide specific results to each manager they collect a small amount of identifying information to be able to determine the division, function, department and team, of the person who has completed it.

Pop! goes the tuft of fur on the top of Colin's head.

"But that seems kind of the opposite of anonymous?" Colin pushes down the tuft of fur on his head. "Especially where's only six of us..."

"I'm afraid I don't control the survey Colin." Bob shrugs in an – it's out of my hands – way. "I only get the results. Alright then," he says. "We need to come up with an action plan for our top three items. I'll read out our results, and we can discuss the main themes." He pauses and looks deliberately at each person. "And also address a few somewhat incorrect beliefs." He flips open the folder and picks up the first page. "Overall, our team score this year is 25%"

"Whoa! Top 25% of the company." Colin smiles broadly. "Nice work Boss."

"Down from 39% last year."

"Oh..." Colin rubs his neck. "Higher is... better. I see. Sorry Boss, please go on."

"Not a problem Colin," Bob says. "I'm confident that this score is clearly a reflection of dissatisfaction with broader company initiatives. Now—"

"No, I'm pretty sure there was a specific section for that," Vanessa says, still trying to move her stuck chair height adjuster.

"I'm sure it influenced it," Bob mutters. "Anyway, the survey company has suggested three areas for us to focus on."

"Exciting," Colin says to Gina and rubs his paws in anticipation.

"I'm not sure I agree with them," Bob snorts and throws up his hands. Colin isn't sure whether it's in annoyance at the situation, or because he's just received an electric shock. "But we're stuck with them." Bob makes a show of deliberately frowning. "Number three, is that we feel our—"

"Systems and processes not supporting us." Graham interrupts. "Again."

Bob glares at him. "Thank you Graham." He holds up the paper. "I've got the results, thank you." He repeats.

Graham holds up a hand. "Sorry, you go."

Bob looks back to the paper. "Number three is that we feel our systems and processes don't support us. Number two, no-one believes anything will change based on the results of this survey. You don't need to mouth along with me Graham." Bob taps the paper into the table. "And this top one, I think is an error, but HR insists that it's not." He shakes his head at the paper and places it back into the folder. "I still think it's wrong, so we'll park it for now." He looks back to the team. "Let's talk about our processes—"

"What was the other one?" Alfred points to the folder. "You didn't tell us number one."

Bob drops back into his chair and waves his hands awkwardly. "Well, it seems pointless, but if you insist." He lifts the paper and mumbles, "I don't trust my manager."

"Sorry what?" Gina lifts her hand to her ear.

Bob huffs. "They said the top result was supposedly that this team said they don't trust their manager." He drops the paper back into the folder and slams it closed.

"Sounds about right." Graham nods.

"Can we see them?" Alfred asks indicating the screen behind Bob. "The results. Rather than you just read them out?"

Bob opens the folder and looks at the comments he had angrily scratched over before the meeting so that no-one else saw them. "That's not really the protocol I'm afraid. And the screen in this room doesn't work. The remote to power it on is missing," he says as the screen springs to life behind him.

"Found it Boss!" Colin says.

"Thanks Colin," Bob says and reluctantly reaches for the cable to connect his computer. After feigning several attempts that there is a problem with the plug, he brings up the detailed results section. "If we're going to look at this," he says, looking around. "There are a couple of comments I'd like to get clarification on, from the person who made them."

"Sorry, one second," Graham holds his hand up. "I think my fuzzy little buddy here..." He turns to Colin. "No offence..."

Colin waves back to say - none taken.

"... raised an important point before, about the survey being anonymous."

"Of course it's anonymous." Bob holds up the folder and shows them where he has written 'Anonymous Annual Survey Results' on the front in red marker. He holds it there for a moment longer, then lets it fall to the table like a mic drop. "Besides, it's simple logic." He taps the folder solidly with two fingers. "If it *wasn't* anonymous, I wouldn't need to ask who made the comments to be able to clarify them. Would I?" He raises his eyebrows and looks around at the team. "So, there's your *proof* it's anonymous."

"You keep using that word," George whispers to Gina in his best Inigo Montoya voice. "I do not think it means what you think it means."

"I'm happy to help clarify mine boss." Colin smiles. "I don't mind. Even though I'd only been here for a few weeks when we filled it out, I tried to make some useful comments."

"Thank you Colin," Bob says. "But as I say, it's anonymous, so I can't tell which ones are yours."

"Oh. Right you are boss. You go ahead and read them, and I'll let you know which ones were mine." Colin sits back and prepares to listen.

"Thank you for your transparency Colin," Bob says. "Hopefully we can all be as transparent as you, to be able to identify where HR misinterpreted people's comments. Although some of them I think are pretty simple to identify..." He narrows his eyes at Brenda.

"I don't know what you're talking about." Brenda leans back into the chair, causing it to roll slowly backwards away from the table. "What the—" She grabs the table and pulls herself forward again.

Bob brings up the results for Question 3 - *I have faith in my manager,* and looks back at her.

"So?" She moves uncomfortably and the chair rolls backwards again. "What's wrong with this chair?" She glares at it as though it will change the chair's attitude.

"Someone had selected Strongly Disagree. And then in the text box for additional comments, created a scale that included an extra option called 'Really Really Strongly Disagree. And selected that."

"There's no way you could identify who that was." Brenda leans forward, causing the chair to roll again. "Stop doing that!" she snarls at it.

"And in the same comments section," Bob continues. "That person also wrote - My manager persecutes me by giving me too much work, and then tries to have me fired just because there happened to be a slow period when I was on leave, and my replacement didn't have enough to do."

"That could have been anyone." Brenda waves him away.

Bob lifts an eyebrow.

"I thought this was supposed to be anonymous," Brenda says, holding the table to stop her chair moving again. "

"It *is* anonymous," Bob says.

"Then how can you accuse me of writing that?" she snorts, and mimes a 'mic-drop' to signify her victory. "It's no wonder I said I didn't trust you."

Bob blinks twice. "Just because it's anonymous doesn't mean I can't make a logical conclusion about who wrote which comments," Bob says looking back at her.

"Anonymous," Vanessa interrupts, reading from the dictionary app on her phone. "One: Of unknown authorship or origin. Two: Not named or identified." She looks up at Bob. "Examples: The people who completed the survey wished to remain anonymous—"

"I know what anonymous means Vanessa..." Bob stares at her.

"I'm not sure you do."

"Anyway, it's not about that," Bob pushes on. "It's about having the trust that my team feel they can come and speak to me about any issues they have." He holds his arms wide to signify that he's there for them. "Everyone knows my door is always open."

"You don't have a door," Gina says.

"I want to be able to have open and respectful conversations," he says ignoring her. "Not have you hide behind..." He lifts the folder. "Some faceless survey."

"It's not *faceless*," Vanessa corrects him. "It's *anonymous*."

"Just to make sure I'm on the same page as you," Graham chimes in. "You're encouraging open and transparent conversation with your team, by pressuring us to own up to the comments that we made in an anonymous survey?"

Bob slumps back and folds him arms. "You're making it sound worse than it is," he pouts. "And I'm not pressuring anyone. I simply believe that if someone has something to say, they should feel that they can come and speak to me about it."

"Seems pretty clear that they can't." Graham shrugs.

"Let's not get into the weeds on this," Bob says quickly and moves to the next section. "The overall comments have been categorised by sentiment into positives and... well, *they* call them negatives. But that makes them sound so... negative." He looks around the table. "I prefer to see them as opportunities for the open and transparent conversation I constantly encourage." He scrolls forward to a picture of a scale titled positive and negative. On each side of the scale are text boxes containing a selection of comments from the survey.

"That looks pretty good boss," Colin says pointing at the heavily weighted positive side. "That one's mine." He says. "My manager is helpful and supportive."

Bob smiles. "Well thank you for that comment Colin. And for your transparency. You see," he says to the others. "It's good to know how Colin feels about our working relationship. If he hadn't told me, I wouldn't have known that comment was from him, because..." He pauses for effect. "It's *anonymous*." He scrunches his face into an – I told you so – look.

"Which is why I also don't know who made that comment on the other side – My manager is an idiot."

"Oh, that was probably me," Graham says. "Although, there might have been other people too."

Bob sits back and stares blankly at him. "Oh, well thank you so much for *your* transparency Graham, by writing that in an anonymous survey." He sneers.

"What?" Graham holds out his hands innocently. "I say that all the time."

"Anyway, let's move on. The next one. My manager is friendly and challenges me to perform to my highest standard."

"Mine too." Colin smiles.

"I thought these were supposed to be positive comments?" Alfred takes off his glasses, looks closely at the lenses and puts them back on. "Why does that say - 'My manager is constantly screwing me over when I ask for a pay rise. Thanks for nothing!'"

"Or that one," Gina points to the screen. "My manager is great at taking credit for my work."

"I saw this in my last job," George says to them, nodding. "The survey program didn't understand sarcasm. So anytime it found a word like 'thanks' or 'great', it thought it was a positive."

"Or 'brilliant' apparently," Graham says, pointing at the next comment. "As in - My manager is brilliant at pretending he's working when he's actually off getting himself a donut."

"Well, *that's* not true," Bob says indignantly.

"I know," Gina agrees. "You're terrible at pretending that."

"My manager is... an imbecile," Vanessa whistles. "That escalated quickly." She keeps reading. "My manager is... Bob smells. What? That one doesn't even make sense."

Colin giggles and quickly covers his mouth.

"Okay I think we're done." Bob yanks the cable out of his computer and the screen goes blank. "I'll send you a curated summary of the comments and speak with each of you individually." He pushes his chair back and storms towards the door. "And I don't smell," he mumbles as he raises his arm to take a quick sniff.

"Wasn't it *his* idea to read the comments?" George shrugs.

"You should never read the comments," Pooja shakes her head.

"That's good advice any time," agrees Colin.

Bing! goes a notification on Colin's computer.

He looks at the five minute reminder for Arthur's extra follow-up: 'Survey results - Brainstorming to identify quick wins and grab the low hanging fruit,' meeting. Colin can see Arthur has added - **Video required!** in bold.

"I definitely want to go to your meeting." He smiles at the Reminder Notification. "It's a double win. Not only do I get to help increase engagement; fruit is my favourite!" He remembers how Mrs Wombat would always tell the class how important fruit was to a healthy diet.

As he's double-checking there is no pre-work (even though he's sure there isn't), a meeting invitation arrives from Poppy in Property. It's addressed to - Floor Champions. "That's odd." Colin scratches his ear. "I don't remember agreeing to anything to do with changes to our floor seating plan..." He checks the time and sees that it clashes with the team stand up. "Maybe I can propose a new time," he says and scrolls through the next few days. "Maybe I could move my weekly one on one with Bob to after the daily stand-up on Tuesday." He checks his calendar to see if it will fit. "Or maybe switch the project update to before the fortnightly planning catch-up; but after the Retro about how we're progressing with Agile." He tries moving a few meetings around again. "If only I could move the weekly all-hands team meeting, or the fortnightly town hall..." He tries a few more different options until it feels too much like he's losing a game of Tetris.

He replies with a tentative yes, and locks his screen and calls over to Graham. "Are you ready for the supplementary meeting to work out why people think they are spending too much time in meetings?" he calls, grabbing his Special Reminder Notebook.

"I think I'll pass," Graham replies walking towards the lift. "I've got priorities." He holds up his plastic re-usable coffee cup that reads – I (heart) my attitude problem.

"I'll fill you in afterwards," Colin says and scoots off to the room. "I want to get there early, before there's only high fruit left." He holds his stomach as it rumbles. "I skipped lunch, so I don't want to miss out," he calls back over his shoulder.

"How was the meeting?" Graham asks, taking a sip of coffee as he walks up to Colin's desk.

"It was amazing!" Colin exclaims, bouncing in his chair.

Graham almost spits his coffee out. "No, I meant Arthur's meeting today," he laughs and wipes his mouth with his sleeve.

"Yes!" Colin nods excitedly. "The extra meeting about spending too much time in meetings, to follow-up on the meeting that ran over last week. Arthur was great."

Graham lifts up Colin's pencil case and pulls out his packet of gum leaves. "Have you had a couple too many of these at lunch?"

"No," Colin laughs, then thinks for a second. "I don't think so. Help yourself by the way."

Graham examines the packet and puts it back. "Thanks, but I'm driving. What do you mean it was great?"

Well," starts Colin. "You know how the meeting was scheduled for an hour?" He shakes his head in awe thinking back to it. "After fifteen minutes... it was over!"

Graham looks around to check if there's a hidden camera and he's on a reality 'Prank TV' show. "You're not seriously telling me that Arthur got through the entire agenda in only fifteen minutes?"

"Oh, no," Colin says. "People kept talking and texting, and Arthur stopped and said if they didn't want to be there and pay attention... that they should leave."

"Bold move," Graham says, perching himself on the edge of Coln's desk. "What happened?"

"Everyone left. There was only me, Mike the Intern and some guy from procurement who's still on probation left, so Arthur said he'd email us the rest of the information, and packed up..." He pauses dramatically. "Successfully reducing a sixty-minute meeting... to only fifteen minutes."

Graham waits in case Colin wants to spread him arms and add a 'Ta da'. "That's certainly an innovative approach," he says, taking a big swig from his cup. "Did you come up with any solutions?"

"No." Colin shakes his head. "That's the *next* meeting," he says, pointing off into the distance.

"Of course it is," Graham says as his eyes follow the direction of Colin's paw.

"The only bad thing..." Colin rubs his middle. "Was that because today's meeting was so quick, I missed out on the fruit." A loud grumble roars up from his stomach.

Graham opens his mouth to ask, 'what fruit?', thinks for a moment, and decides to let it go. "I'm just glad this survey rubbish is over for another year."

Bing! goes the email on Colin's computer. Bing! comes another. Bing! Bing! Bing! "Someone's popular." Graham nods as two more meeting invitations appear in Colin's Inbox.

"It's not just me." Colin smiles, clicking to accept each one. "You're popular too. These are the invitations for the workshops to brainstorm the remainder of the opportunities, and schedule meetings to develop Action Plans!" He clicks to accept another one.

"You mean *I'm* getting these as well?" Graham leans forward to read the subject line – Seven tips to increase meeting effectiveness, Workshop 1 of 9. "I need a coffee." He squeezes his eyes closed.

"You've got a coffee." Colin points to Graham's re-usable cup that reads - If I agreed with you, we'd both be stupid.

Graham tilts back his head and drains the rest of his cup. "I don't think you can have too much coffee," he says.

Colin watches Graham's left eyebrow twitch like a caterpillar on a treadmill. "I'm not sure that's true," he says rubbing his chin. "Okay," He decides. "Give me a sec to accept these while they're hot." He clicks another invitation and realises it clashes with the pre-meeting to get ready for the discussion to prepare for the Reporting Wrap-up session.

POP! goes the tuft of fur on the top of Colin's head.

"Hmm," he says as he tries to smooth it back down. "Maybe I'll catch up," he says to Graham over his shoulder as another invite for a 'Floor Champions' meeting arrives, making him triple-booked. "I have a feeling this might take longer than I thought."

Efficiency = Flexibilty + Resilience
x KOALA

"Who's that sitting next to Bob?" Brenda says, turning to Bill. Before he can answer, she turns back and calls out to Bob. "Who's that sitting next to you?" She makes a show of looking confused. "Is she here to fix the air conditioning?" Brenda grumbles. "I can't believe they haven't fixed the air conditioning in this room yet." She wipes her arm dramatically across her forehead to clear the sweat from her eyes, even though there's none there. "You know it's rude not to introduce people when a meeting starts." She tuts and looks around for support.

When she realises no-one is paying attention to her, she slumps back into her chair and folds her arms. "At least *I* think it is," she adds sulkily. "No excuse for rudeness," she mutters to herself.

Bob clears his throat. "When people stop chattering," he glares at Brenda. "I'll be able to actually *start* the meeting," he says trying to keep his voice even. "And then I'll be able to *tell you* who this is."

Brenda points to the small, yellow metal box on the table in front of the mystery woman. "And what's in the box?"

"If you'll let me—"

"I shouldn't need to have to point it out to you," Brenda calls back, secure that without her input, the mystery of who is sitting next to Bob would remain forever unsolved.

"Is this *another* agile thing?" Gina whines, glancing up from her phone.

"No. It's not another agile thing," Bob assures her quickly.

"I thought we were done with that agile rubbish?" Graham says and takes a sip from his plastic re-usable coffee cup that reads - 'What made you think I was vaguely interested in what you're saying'.

"We are," Bob the Boss replies, then adds quickly. "I mean, were not *done*," he pauses, then adds again. "And it's *not* rubbish," he sighs and rubs his forehead. "Anyway, I just said less than five seconds ago that this *isn't* agile—"

"Right. So we *are* done with agile." Graham nods and puts his cup on the table.

"No, we're not *done* with agile." Bob glares at him. "It's just that we launched agile *last* month, and now we're on to the next—"

"Flavour of the month," Graham finishes for him.

"Initiative," Bob continues slowly, ignoring Graham's input.

"I quite liked those two agile people we had here," Bill muses. "What were their names again?" He taps his chin, ignoring Bob's cough for him to stop. "I think the young fellow was Kim? But I can't recall the lady's name..."

"Hmm," Vanessa says, hiding a mischievous smirk. "Yes... I can almost picture them sitting just there." She looks over towards the front of the room. "Oh my gosh, what *was* her name again?" she says in mock exasperation, pretending to look confused.

Bob gives her a 'I know what you're doing - and it's not funny' stare. "It was *Kim*," he says firmly, and adds a 'stop encouraging him' sneer. "Now if I can—"

"Yes yes, that was the fellow's name." Bill nods and scratches his head. "It's the young *lady's* that I can't recall."

"I'm not sure about the guy." George leans forward and furrows his brow. "But I thought *her* name Kym?"

"No, no." Bill says, shaking his head definitively. "I'm sure it was the young *man* who's name was Kim."

"Oh for God's sake," Bob snaps and slaps his hands on the table, causing his visitor to jump. "They were *both* named Kim."

"Of course!" Vanessa throws her arms up theatrically. "That's right." She taps her finger against her head as though it should have been obvious. "How silly of me—"

"Really?" Bill turns between her and Bob. "Both Kim." He frowns and nods to himself. "What an odd coincidence. You know—"

"Now if we can move on," Bob jumps in before Bill can get going again. "Today—"

"Whatever happened to Kim and Kym?" Graham interrupts. "Aren't they doing this agile stuff anymore? That's a shame."

Colin shrugs back.

Brenda makes a show of checking her watch. "I don't have time for this. We've been here five minutes and you still haven't introduced Kim from agile yet." She huffs. "Or told us what's in the box?"

"It's not Kim," Bob sighs and rubs his forehead. "And she's not agile." He looks up and glances at the woman sitting next to him. "Well, she might be, but not in a--"

"Is she important then?" Brenda snaps. "I've got things to do. The Finance All-Hands Meeting is coming up next week."

"Yes, she *is* important," Bob sneers at Brenda and turns to his visitor apologetically. "Sorry, about that, we—" he suddenly stops. "Wait." He turns back to Brenda. "What does the Finance meeting have to do with you?"

125

"Who else is supposed to design the Scavenger Hunt?" she replies. "*They're* obviously not going to. So *of course* it's up to me again." She rolls her eyes. "As usual. Because I have to do everything around here—"

Bob holds up his hand. "Let's take this offline," he says and wonders whether he should have just stayed in bed. "Now, if I can finally begin the meeting." He glares at Brenda. "This, is—"

"Kim?" Gina calls out.

"No!" Bob growls. "Enough with the Kims! I don't want to hear anyone mention a 'Kim' again in this meeting." He puts his hands on the table and leans forward. "This..." He sits back and motions to the woman next to him. "Is *Kim*— shit! No! It's Poppy." He squeezes his eyes shut for a few seconds and takes a breath. "From Property," he says, opening them again slowly. "This, is Poppy, from Property. And Poppy is here today, to talk about raising workplace efficiency and increasing staff engagement, and—"

Poppy suddenly leaps out of the chair. "Workplace flexibility!" she declares loudly and claps twice, causing Brenda and George to jump.

Poppy moves carefully across to the empty space at the front of the room, as though she is following a pre-defined path to the centre of the main stage at the Opera House. She stops; spreads her arms wide; and holds herself in place for a beat. "How flexible are you?" She points to George.

"I'm more focused on strength," George replies. "But I can touch my toes." He pushes his chair back to stand up.

Bob waves at him to sit back down. "There's no need to demonstrate," he says, making it clear it's a non-event. "Everyone can touch their toes."

"*Touch* them?" Graham laughs, patting his stomach. "I don't even remember what mine look like."

Colin looks down and wiggles his own toes. "I think I'd miss mine if I couldn't see them." He frowns.

Poppy claps again to get their attention back. "I'd like everyone to stand up please."

George points at Bob. "He just said that we weren't demonstrating—"

"Is this where everyone *usually* sits for this meeting?" Poppy says moving her gaze from one side of the room to the other to signify she's taking in everyone the room, but instead it looks more like she's following an invisible tennis match happening behind them.

"Sure, I think so," Bob replies, taking a guess that she's talking to him.

Poppy bends her knees and squats. She pushes her arms out towards them with her palms face up. "I'd like everyone to stand up please," she says, making it sound more like a statement than a request, and slowly raises her arms upwards.

I reminds Colin of the time at school talent show, when his friend Joey the joey had pretended to be a magician. His big finish was to make Patty Platypus float magically across the stage, and he had lifted his arms in the same way. Unfortunately, he'd forgotten to tell Patty, and so he just ended up accidently pushing her into the front row.

Brenda leans back in her chair. "I'm not doing anything until someone tells me what's in the box," she says.

"Like... *stand up*, stand up?" Pooja points upwards.

"Bob said we don't really need to stand up for a Stand Up." Graham leans back and folds his arms. "And I thought you said this wasn't agile?"

Bob claps his hands quickly. "Okay people. Up." He pushes himself out of the chair. "I can take the lead on this one." He smiles at Poppy. "Come on, come on." He claps again. "It's not that hard."

"That's what she said," Graham calls out proudly, and takes a celebratory sip of coffee.

Colin lifts his paw to cover up his giggling and pops off his chair. He stands to attention with his arms by his sides. "Just like assembly at school," he smiles up at Poppy and nods.

The others slowly make their way to their feet and stand awkwardly in front of their chairs.

"I don't see how this is making make me more productive," Gina says, pushing herself out of her chair.

"Or engaged," George adds.

"The first step to improved efficiency," Poppy announces, and begins pacing across the room like a General addressing her troops before sending them into battle. "Is to change our mindset." She stops and

129

spins forward again. Her gaze rejoins the invisible tennis match at the back of the room. "If we continue to do things the same way, we will continue to achieve the same results."

"That's exactly right," Bob adds, as if he's suddenly now a key partner with Poppy in this discussion. "The definition of insanity." He taps his head knowingly and nods to the team. He waits for a moment while they look back at him blankly, then turns to Poppy, as though he's made his point and is handing back to her.

"Uh, yes. Thank you," Poppy says. "Now as I was—" She stops, noticing Bill has his hand raised. "Yes, do you have a question?" she asks. "And you don't need to raise your hand."

"I believe it's when someone has lost touch with reality," Bill declares and nods towards Bob.

Poppy looks blankly between them. "Sorry?"

"He just asked what the definition of insanity was," Bill replies, pointing at Bob. He looks up thoughtfully. "I'd need to confirm that exactly in a dictionary of course, but for the purpose of this meeting, I feel that should suffice."

Bob rubs his eyes and enjoys the darkness for a moment. "I wasn't *asking*—"

"I must say, I'm slightly concerned if insanity is our topic for this meeting," Bill adds, with a look of concern.

"It's not our topic," Bob stops him. "I was just supporting and expanding on what Kim—"

"Poppy," Colin corrects him.

"Yes?" Poppy says.

Colin waves past her. "No no. Sorry, Bob just called you Kim. I was just helping correct him."

Bob shakes his head. "No, I don't think I did."

"You did," Pooja agrees.

"Yep," George and Gina chime in.

"I don't believe I did, but..." Bob holds his hands up in false resignation. "If *everyone* thinks so..." he says in the same way the hero in a pantomime does when the audience yells out – 'He's behind you!'

"Sounds like you could use a little sanity of your own!" Bill laughs. "Reminds me of my time in the army. No such thing as insanity back then," he nods. "Unless you were in charge I suppose. Back then you just pushed everything down inside." He reflects fondly. "I do remember one poor young chap, Alex, I believe his name was..." He taps his chin for a moment and frowns. "Or maybe Sam—"

"Let's take this offline," Bob tries to interrupt.

"Poor Sam." Bill barrels on. "Ended up in hospital, endlessly drawing cartoons." He shakes his head sadly.

"I like cartoons," Colin says, supporting Bill's story. "They make me smile and brighten my day."

"Oh, no," Bill says, his voice growing deeper as he shakes his head solemnly. "These weren't funny cartoons. *Sam* thought they were funny, but no... not amusing at all..." he trails off, lost in his thoughts.

Poppy waits for a few moments, unsure what her next step should be. She looks over to Bob for direction.

"Just push on." Bob nods to continue.

"Uh, right." Poppy begins. "Where were we?" Oh yes—"

"He'd draw them on the walls you see," Bill interrupts, as though there hadn't been a break in his conversation. "The poor nurses spent more time cleaning the walls than anything else." He looks at

Poppy. "You would know, being from Property and all that."

"Uh, yes," Poppy agrees slowly, unsure how to respond. "I'm sure ink must be difficult to remove."

"Ink?" Bill replies. "Oh, not ink," he says, then adds casually, "Faeces."

"Jesus Bill!" Bob throws up his hands.

"Oh my god," Poppy, gasps and wraps her arms tightly around her chest and shoulders.

Gina gasps and stares at him wide-eyed. "You knew a man who drew cartoons that weren't funny on a wall... with his own shit?" she asks with her hand covering her mouth.

"I didn't know Leunig was in the army," Graham says.

Poppy pulls out a bottle of water from her bag and takes a huge gulp.

Bill thinks for a moment. "I'm not sure if it was ever really confirmed whether it was *all* his own." Bill rubs his chin thoughtfully. "He *was* oddly prolific now I come to think about it."

"That's horrific in so many ways." Bob stares at him in disbelief. Somewhere he hears a small dry retch. "Why would you tell us something like that?"

"Is that what's in the box?" Brenda calls out, leaning forward on her chair.

"Maybe we should take a break?" Graham tips his cup upside down to show that it's empty.

"No," Bob says trying to claw back at least a veneer of order. He lifts his hand to his temple and pushes his thumbs into the small dent in the flesh. "Please Poppy, go on," he says, determined to ride it out until the end.

"Well—" she begins. Her voice cracks and she takes another long swig from her water bottle. "Uh..." She looks around. "Oh, can everybody stand up again please?"

"We just did this," Brenda sighs and noisily thumps the chair around as she stands up. "Am I in church now?"

"No-one told you to sit back down," Bob sneers.

Brenda points at Graham accusingly. "He didn't even stand up!"

"Okay," Poppy begins again, trying to regain a semblance of control. "I'd like you all to move to a different seat." She motions for them to move. "By changing our seat..." she says dramatically. "We change our thoughts. And those new thoughts make us more engaged. And when we're more engaged, we're more efficient."

"Alright!" Colin yells and bounces across to the nearest empty chair. "I'm always up for ways to be more efficient!"

"Thank you," Bob acknowledges him.

"Wait," Colin stops suddenly and looks over at Gina's chair on the other side of the table. "Do I become even *more* efficient if I move *even further* away?" He races across the room.

"My house is even *further* away," Graham says raising his hand. "I could stay there and shoot my efficiency through the roof."

"Can we all follow Colin's example and quickly find a new spot please." Bob claps twice mimicking Poppy.

"This reminds me of the time—" Bill begins.

"Silently," Bob interrupts and waves his hands quickly to hurry them along.

The team heave a collective sigh and awkwardly bump into each other as they navigate their way through the small area.

Colin climbs up into his new chair and watches the team meander slowly around the room, until eventually they all end up one chair to the right of their original one, and sit down.

Graham walks twice in a small circle and returns to the same seat as before.

"Thank you," Poppy says. "Now that we are all focused and energised," she continues, ignoring the fidgeting while everyone tries to readjust their chairs. "I'd like to announce our new Workplace Efficiency Platform."

"Yay!" Colin yells. "That sounds exciting! Where will it go?" He pushes himself up in the chair and strains to look out into the main office area. "We used to have a big platform at the front of our assembly hall in school." He turns to Bob. "Will you use it for presenting certificates and awards?"

"Uh, no," Poppy says slowly and wonders whether her roommate had slipped one of their special mushrooms into her sandwich as a prank. "It's not a physical platform. It's a *metaphorical* platform." She steps over to Colin. "It's a platform…" she lowers her voice and leans forward dramatically. "*Of efficiency.*"

"Ohhh." Colin stares up at her in awe.

Poppy goes on to explain that a key part of the new Workplace Efficiency Platform is to stop people being forced to sit at the same old boring desk. She pulls her mouth into an exaggerated frown, and in a voice that sounds like a child who's been told they have to clean their room before they can watch Saw again adds, "Every single day."

"But my desk isn't boring. It's… old, maybe not as old as him," she says pointing at Bob. "But I like my desk," Vanessa counters. Everyone murmurs supportively and nods in agreement.

Poppy looks them over in a way that reminds Colin of the time Mrs Wombat had told the class that just because you *can* do something, doesn't always mean that you *should*, right before she removed any projects that required glue, for the remainder of the year.

Poppy crouches down and paints on a smile. She explains to them that by not being tied to *one* desk, every morning would become a new and exciting adventure. It meant they were free to work from anywhere that took their fancy.

"But what do I do with my photos, and firefighter calendar... And my stress ball, my Jesus Saves money box, and my—" Umi asks concerned.

George raises his hand. "And what about my novelty desktop drum kit—"

"Each of you will have a locker for your computer, and for any other essentials you want to keep in the office." Poppy forges on, raising her volume to talk louder than the others.

Pooja nods. "That sounds quite good actually. I've probably got too much on my desk. It would be good to declutter."

"I've read that book too!" Umi smiles. "I got rid of all the things that didn't bring me joy."

"Does it include people as well?" Graham calls out.

"Can we keep to the topic please?" interrupts Bob, rubbing his temple.

"Ridiculous," Brenda snorts derisively. "How can I keep my computer inside a locker overnight. It's going to overheat and break." Brenda gives the equivalent of a 'checkmate' huff. "I don't have time to call the Help Desk every time it won't work."

Colin shudders involuntarily when Brenda says – Help Desk.

"Obviously you'll need to shut down your computer each day, the way you do now, before you put it away," Poppy explains slowly, wondering if she'll ever find her way back to the real world.

"Turn it off?" Brenda scoffs. "I don't have time to turn it off, it takes forever. There's always some kind of stupid update. I don't know about *this lot...*" She jabs her thumb over her shoulder. "But *I* don't have time for that."

Gina puts her hands on her cheeks in pretend shock and mouths - '*This lot*' - to Vanessa.

"Me too," Umi agrees. "It takes far too long for it to shut down. I'd miss my train."

"You're supposed to shut down at least every week," Alfred says. "That's how all the software gets updated from IT."

"My software is fine." Brenda waves her hand dismissively. "I don't know why they keep changing it.

One minute the button is here, the next minute it's over there then it's on a different screen—"

"Let's not get off track," Bob jumps in before Brenda can get her rant into second gear. "While I'm with you 100% on this initiative Poppy, I am going to have to agree with the team on this one. The computers do take a bit of time to shut down and start up."

Poppy mechanically turns to Bob and smiles. "I appreciate your feedback," she says in a way that clearly suggests she doesn't. "However, the research indicates that starting and stopping a computer adds up to a combined total of only 3.4 minutes per day." She smiles as though she is providing the secret to enlightenment. "And I'm sure we can all spare an extra 3.4 minutes out of 24 hours."

"Three minutes?" George looks at Vanessa in disbelief. "Am I the only person whose computer takes at least *ten* minutes just to start?"

"Yep. Mine does too," Gina agrees. "And at least that, or more, to shut down."

"Mine too," Graham agrees strongly to support his team, even though he hasn't shut down for so long, he's not sure where the button is anymore. He wiggles his cup at Poppy and tips it upside down again, hinting for a break.

"The Property team have spent a long time studying the research around flexible working and efficiency," Poppy says, ignoring the drops of coffee dripping onto the carpet from Graham's cup. "It will take a few days, but once you get used to it, you'll be coming to ask Bob here for more work." She smiles broadly. "Yes, you have a comment?" She points at Alfred. "You don't need to raise your hand."

"May I ask a clarifying question?" Alfred asks, and continues before Bob can say 'no'. "You're saying, that setting up my computer, keyboard and mouse; adjusting my chair and monitors so they're ergonomically correct, waiting the, what did we decide it was… ten minutes?" He pauses. "Ten minutes, for it to start, and then packing up again at the end of the day," he pauses for effect. "Is going to make me *more* efficient?"

"Yes." Poppy smiles, pleased that Alfred is on board and understands.

Alfred scratches his beard. "More efficient than just sitting down at the same desk every day and logging in to my computer?"

"Yes," Poppy agrees as though she has just been asked to make a call on whether water is wet.

POP! goes the tuft of fur on the top of Colin's head.

"And now, if there's no more questions, I have a present for each of you!" Poppy reaches down and picks up the yellow metal box from the table.

"Finally they listen!" Brenda throws her arms up.

Poppy looks between Brenda and Bob. He nods for her to press on and she smooths out her shirt awkwardly. "It's your locker assignments, and keys." She stumbles, then beams at them like they've won the lottery. "Bob? Would you like to do the honours and hand them out?"

Bob reaches over and opens the box. He produces a small key with a yellow tag, and holds it high above his head, as though it's an Olympic gold medal. He jiggles it a few times enticingly, then drop sit back into the box with clunk. "Come up when I call your name," he says and shakes the box vigorously, causing the keys to bounce and clatter loudly in the metal tin. "This is how you build team engagement and buy-in," he whispers to Poppy from the corner of his mouth, and pushes the box across the table towards the team. It slides an arm's length forward, leaving a deep scar in the tabletop. "That was already there," Bob says quickly and snatches the assignment list from Poppy's hands. "I think that because *Colin* is being so positive about this initiative. He should be our first cap off the rack."

"Oh," Poppy apologises to Colin. "Sorry. We don't have anywhere for hats." She shakes her head. "Or coats," she adds. "Or umbrellas, raincoats, wet shoes, backpacks..."

Colin slides off his chair and bounces excitedly up to the table. He holds his paw up to his mouth and whispers to Poppy. "He means - cab off the rank," he says as he thanks Bob for the key and races back to his seat.

"Thanks Colin," Bob smiles and looks back to the sheet. "Graham," he calls.

"What?" Graham says looking up from his phone.

"Your key," Bob nods towards the tin.

"Don't think so," Graham says reaching into his pocket. "Nope. Not mine." He pulls his keys from his pants pocket and jingles them.

Bob drops the paper onto the desk. "Maybe I did something in a past life..." he mutters to himself and leans across the table to grab the tin. He catches the edge with his fingertips and pulls it back towards him. The corner leaves another deep gouge in the wood. Bob sighs and pulls out Graham key. "Can you pass that to Graham please?" he says handing it to Gina, and picks up the next one. "Bill."

"Present!" Bill snaps.

"Here you go." Bob swings his arm back. "Think fast old timer." He winks at Poppy and tosses the key to Bill. It sails majestically, falls short, bounces off the table onto George's thigh, and slips onto the floor.

"Is this mine or Bill's?" George says, leaning forward to pick it up.

"You know..." Bill says. "This reminds me of the time my wife and I were invited to a neighbourhood party." He takes the key from George and examines it. "Each guest had to drop their keys into a bowl as they came in. And then after a few drinks people would take turns pulling a key from the bowl and—"

"No!" Gina, Vanessa and Bob all yell at once.

Bill frowns and puts his key into his pocket.

"Vanessa," Bob calls, throwing her key to her.

"Ow!" she yells. "That hit me on the head."

Bob looks over at Poppy and shrugs apologising for the lacklustre skills of his team. "Apparently catching is a lost art," he says. "Gina, can you please pass these out?" He puts the tin on top of the assignment list and launches it across the table. It slides smoothly past Gina, Vanessa, Brenda and Bill, and spills off the edge and onto the floor with a crash.

"Really?" Bob stares at them as the keys and tags bounce across the carpet. "No-one could put their hand out?" he says as they all stare back blankly. "Can everyone just grab their keys please."

"I don't seem to have a key," Bill raises his hand after they have all been collected.

"You've got your key already!" Bob lifts his hand and pushes his thumb softly into his temple. "It's in your pocket."

"Ah," Bill checks. "So it is." He holds it up. "What does L26, E, U32 mean?"

"Excellent question," Poppy replies, pleased to be able to get back on a semblance of a track, even though she suspects the track is heading towards a dead end. "It's the location of your locker. L26 is level Twenty-Six, E is the East locker bank, U is for the upper row, and 32 is your locker number."

"Which way is East?" Bill looks around.

"I've got a compass," Colin says helpfully. "I can check for you." He opens the zipper on his pencil case.

"I think my tag must be wrong," Pooja says, holding hers up. "It says level 27, and I work on level 26,"

"Yes," Poppy nods seriously. "We are aware that in some cases, there wasn't an adequate number of lockers located on the same floor as the locker owners," she explains. "But," she gushes, "it's only a short trip to the next floor," she pauses for effect. "And it's actually a double-win for you, because we all know that walking more is an added health benefit."

Colin raises his paw. "My tag says Upper," he says looking down at his little legs. "I'm wondering if I should have a Lower locker?"

Poppy lips move into the type of forced smile that comes from answering this question more times than she would wish on her worst enemy. She rapidly states that all the lockers have already been allocated, and delivers a well-rehearsed monologue covering how everyone works through change at their own pace, that he should give it a chance, and that in the unlikely event that he still had concerns after a few months, she would see if she could move him to a spare locker on level 38, near the construction area.

"Okay, does everyone have their key?" Bob says, checking his watch and calculating that he has time to get to and from the donut shop before his next meeting if he wraps up in the next two minutes. "Great, if there's no more questions, let's wrap it up." He stands up and begins walking to the door.

"I'm quite excited to be a part of this initiative," Colin says. "Thanks Poppy." He raises his paws and begins a round of applause for her. "I can't wait to be more efficient."

147

Bob stops and awkwardly turns. "Yes..." He joins in the applause and reluctantly steps back toward her. "Let's thank Kim— Poppy, for her time today." He claps more loudly to try and imply that he is the one to rally the troops behind it. "And we look forward to beginning our new efficient way of working when it's eventually launched." He turns back to the door. "Look forward to hearing the next steps."

"What do you mean?" Poppy turns to him as he moves towards the door. "It starts on Monday. Yours is the last team I'm handing out keys to."

The applause abruptly stops, and a collective gasp erupts from the team.

Poppy turns to back them. "Surely you've all seen the communications kits and launch schedule?" she says and rejoins the invisible tennis match behind them.

"Launch schedule?"

"Communications kit?"

"Yes," Poppy says. "Bob receives regular updates on progress."

Bob realises he's the only one still clapping and slowly stops. "I think you might need to check your distribution list," Bob says and laughs at the ridiculousness of yet another failed change program. "I don't believe I've *ever* received one of those." He rolls his eyes to Gina and mouths, "Typical."

"No, here you are here," Poppy says, showing him the communications dashboard. "And you also attended the learning workshop three weeks ago."

"I think there's a mistake in your system," Bob twitches awkwardly and tries to laugh it off, vaguely remembering signing into something and immediately excusing himself to go home early. "I don't recall a..." He rubs the back of his neck. "What was it?" he asks again. "A *Workshop*?" he says, rolling it around on his tongue, as though it's a not a word he's familiar with.

"I'm sorry," Vanessa leans forward. "You're not trying to tell me that you're expecting this to happen..." She looks around at the other confused faces. "Next Monday?"

"Yay!" Colin says and bounces excitedly.

"That's far too soon," George shakes his head. "It's not really fair to spring this on us at three o'clock on a Friday," he says as though he's hoping to win the crown for understatement of the century.

"I don't have time to pack up all my things this afternoon." Brenda sits up angrily, flailing her key. "And I bet this so-called *locker* of yours, isn't going to be big enough to fit my photo booth props and emergency dance floor." She folds her arms and thumps heavily back in the chair, causing it to creak in protest.

Bob moves slowly back to the centre of the room. "Let's not focus on the mistakes of others," he says, continuing his attempt to divert blame to Poppy's communication plan. He clasps his hands in front of him, and slowly tilts his head, as though he's a preacher about to provide a eulogy. "As Poppy said, it's common for people to resist change," he says softly, hoping to sound compassionate, but coming across more as condescending. "It's only natural to fear something new." He tilts his head to the other side. "I understand how you're feeling." He pauses and looks around the room, confident his sincerity and empathy have them in the palm of his hand.

He waits another beat and glances over his shoulder to make sure Poppy isn't within hearing distance and raises his hand to his mouth and whispers. "Especially when the people behind the change haven't managed it well."

"I think I speak for everyone," Graham says, standing up. "When I say that for us to add value to this important initiative..." He nods sagely to show his support. "That it's important that we all have the opportunity to fully understand our role in it, and take the time to be properly organised and prepared." He holds out his hands to the team who nod and murmur agreement. "I think if Poppy could come back in say... three..." He looks up to the ceiling for a moment and rubs his chin thoughtfully. "Maybe six... months. We'll be right behind her."

Poppy snatches up her water bottle and takes a huge swig. "It starts Monday," she turns and says flatly to Bob. "You should have your team take some time today to familiarise yourselves with where their lockers are and how they work."

"I feel more efficient already!" Colin yells excitedly. "I can't wait until Monday."

Colin bounces excitedly through the almost empty lobby and waves good morning to the security guard as passes by. He's glad that he set his alarm to arrive early and be ready for his first day working flexibly. "This is very different to my first day," he says to himself and scans his security pass. He thinks back to that day: The river of people coming in, how he had to move diagonally like he was swimming to the side of a river, to get to the reception area. Today, he strides straight past reception and turns into the lift lobby. "Hi!" he says to two other early starters. "I'm Colin." He glances at their security passes. "Hi Margaret. Hi Brad," he says bouncing from one foot to the other.

"Hello Colin," Maragret says, and points towards the reception area. "There's a toilet just over there."

Colin laughs. "Thanks, but I'm just excited! It's flexi-desking day today." He bounces some more, as the lift doors ding open.

Brad steps past Colin and Margaret with the misplaced confidence of someone who thinks they're cool, but everyone else considers a massive dick, and leans casually against the wall in front of the lift panel.

"We did that last week," he scoffs, without looking up from his phone.

Colin motions - after you - to Margaret, then follows her in. "Is everyone much more productive and efficient now?" Colin asks expectantly.

"What? Of course not," Brad snorts, scrolling to the next meme. "I didn't move," he laughs. "I just said we did. Property are too stupid to know."

"Well that would explain why there were no efficiency gains," Colin says, politely pointing past Brad at the floor buttons.

"Can someone..." Margaret says, looking directly at Brad. "Press 14 please?"

Colin waits for Brad to acknowledge her or move, but instead he moves his thumb to scroll to the next video. "Can you press 14 and 26 please..." Colin motions toward the panel again as the lift doors begin to close. Colin reaches his paw past Brad and pushes the button for 14, then stretches on tippy-toes to just reach 26. "Never mind," he says. "I've got it."

Brad looks at Colin, then at the lift panel as though he's never seen one before, and returns to his social media feed.

"Thank you," Margaret says. "We're starting flexible desking today too. I'm not sure I'm convinced to be honest. It feels a bit too much like musical chairs for me." She wrings her hands uncertainly.

"Ooh. I like musical chairs," Colin smiles, feeling his anticipation rise even further.

"More like last man standing," Brad grunts distractedly. "The only reason I'm here this early is some of my team said they'd make me work from the kitchen if I didn't move this week."

"I didn't know we made food here," Colin says as the lift dings for 14 and the doors slide open.

"Well, this is me. Enjoy your flexi-desking Colin." Margaret waves, stepping forward.

"They're joking obviously," Brad snorts and pushes himself off the wall in front of her. "I can do whatever I want." He oozes out through the doors.

"Obviously," Margaret winks at Colin. "You wouldn't want to have to come in early to avoid working from the kitchen." She stops and waits politely until he is out of the way.

Colin giggles. "Have a great day!" He waves, then makes a point to add, "Margaret!" He presses the door close button and watches Brad suddenly look up, confused. Colin hears him call out - Hold the lift, this isn't my floor, as the doors close with a satisfying clunk.

Colin follows lift protocol and watches the floor numbers as he runs through his plan to seek out the best desk to achieve maximum efficiency. He zips out before the doors are even fully open and races to his locker. He pulls out his key and cranes his head up towards the upper row. "Let's do this." He puts the key between his teeth and reaches up to grab the top of the 'Never put our staff in danger' sign as a handhold. He swings up to the top of a pot plant stand, and hoists himself up on top of the locker bank. He moves carefully to above his locker, digs his back claws into the wood so he doesn't topple off, leans over and slides the key into the lock. He reaches in one by one and grabs the essentials - his computer, pencil case and Special Reminder notebook. He stretches for his coffee cup, but it's just out of reach, and he decides to come back later to collect the rest of his items, when Graham is here to help.

He carefully drops his notebook and pencil case to the ground, balances his computer on the top of the Safety-First Suggestion Box and climbs down. "Take that Ethan Hunt." He retrieves items and walks over to his usual desk.

He stops in front of it and smiles. He straightens the right-hand monitor for the next person. It sits there for a few seconds, before slowly drooping back onto an angle again. He moves his paw slowly across the desktop and thanks it for the good times they've had together since his first day. Then leans in close and whispers. "This isn't goodbye. I'll come back and sit with you again," he promises. "But flexibly, sometime in the future."

He steps back and wishes his desk good luck, takes a deep breath and strides to the opposite end of what Poppy had called - 'Bob's Border', to find a desk as far away from his usual one as he can, for maximum efficiency.

He holds out his paw like a water diviner and hovers it over the line of identical grey desks. "Best desk is…" He moves slowly forward, and is drawn towards the corner desk that faces the main corridor.

He holds his paw over it. "Good overall space," he says. "But maybe too many distractions." He imagines the hustle and bustle of people walking past.

He moves along the desks to the right and finds one with a heart scratched into it. "Will you look at that," he says. "This one is perfect!" He high-fives himself, climbs up on the chair and plugs his computer in, ready to amp up his effectiveness. While his computer goes through its start-up routine, he carefully organises his pencil case and Special Reminder Notebook next to his computer, and out of habit, adjusts the right monitor to an upward angle. When it stays there, he laughs quietly to himself and moves it back. "Looks like it's going to take a while to get used to the new digs," he says reaching for the height adjuster on the chair. He feels around a bit, but still nothing. He climbs down and discovers that the height adjustment lever has been snapped off and wedged into a gap in the backrest. "Hmm," he says. "I'll need to take you to the repair station." And set off down the corridor, pushing the chair in front of him.

Graham had helpfully told him on his first day, that if there was ever a problem with his chair, just take it to a meeting room and swap it for one that isn't broken. Colin wasn't sure how the people who fixed the chairs knew when someone had dropped one off, but he knew he didn't have any koala-fications in managing chair repairs.

He tries a few of the replacement chairs until he finds one that works. "Gosh," he says pushing it back to his desk. "This is giving me an entirely new perspective of the office." He nearly trips when a wheel snags on a worn spot in the carpet, and he lifts it over carefully. "Hi new desk, I'm back," he says and adjusts the chair. "Okay computer." He rubs his paws together expectantly, ready to login. "Let's get this extra efficiency going! Oh." He frowns looking at the Loading screen. "You're still starting."

Colin sits back and looks around the office again, taking in the new sights. He covers his mouth to hide his smile at the glasses and devil horns someone has drawn on the picture of the CEO. He takes note of the direction of the photocopy room and mentally tries to estimate the number of steps to the lift. He spins the chair around and looks behind him at a poster of a cat holding onto a rope with the caption – Hang in there.

"You can do it buddy." He gives a supportive fist pump and looks back at the Loading screen. He frowns and straightens his pencil case and checks his Special Reminder notebook for any important notes he may have forgotten about, but can't find any. He carefully places it back, and moves it in line with the keyboard again, carefully lines the computer up under the monitor.

He taps his claws on the desk and re-adjusts his pencil case again. "Hmm. Maybe this is a good opportunity to clear you out," he says opening the zip and tipping everything out onto his desk. He starts sorting through the pens, pencils, markers and gum leaves, when his fur bristles from a sound behind him. He lifts an ear and listens to what he's sure is the mindless shuffling coming from the hallway behind him. He gulps and wishes he hadn't stayed up late to watch the zombie movie on Saturday. He closes his eyes and hears a soulless voice moan from around the corner - I need coffee.

Colin jerks his eyes open. "Graham? You're early too!" He beams. "Extra keen for more efficiency?"

"Misread the bloody clock when I woke up didn't I?" Graham huffs. "Couldn't work out why the traffic was so light."

Colin smiles. "Where are you going to sit today?"

"Hmm." Graham rubs his chin and scans the empty office. "I thought I might try that one over there," he says, pointing to his usual desk.

"Oh Graham, you're such a kidder." Colin laughs. "If you don't move, how will you be more efficient?"

"Don't know how I could be." Graham shrugs and holds up his plastic re-usable coffee cup that reads - 'If I knew what I was doing I wouldn't be here'. "Shall we?"

"Sure," Colin says. "I'm okay to wait while you find the right desk that will maximise your output, and get yourself set up."

Graham glances disinterestedly around the vacant desks and drops his bag onto the one next to Colin's. "Done. Let's go."

Colin slides down from his chair. "Are you sure you don't want to turn on your computer first? Mine's taking a while to start up."

"I'll take a while to start up if I don't get coffee into me," Graham grumbles as they walk off towards the lift.

Colin giggles and presses the Down button. He politely steps back out when the doors open and says 'Hi!' to each person as they step out.

After what seems like a hundred 'Hi's' he takes a breath. "How many people do these lifts hold?" he says. "It's like one of those clown cars at the circus." He rocks his head from side to side. "Di-di-diddle-liddle-di-di-do-do." He sings the carnival song.

"Speaking of clowns," Graham says, nodding towards the final person to step out.

"Morning Boss!" Colin smiles as Bob steps out. "I'm all set up at my new desk."

Bob stops and frowns. "New desk?"

"Ha!" Colin laughs. "Nice try Boss. As if *you* don't remember it's flexi-desking day."

Bob blinks twice as he realises he had forgotten to pack his computer and other items into his locker on Friday because he'd snuck out for a donut. He gulps. "Yes!" he says. "Can't fool you Colin." He raises himself up on his toes and looks hopefully over to his desk... Empty. "Shit," he mumbles under his breath and tries to remember what Poppy said would happen to anything left behind at the end of the day. "Good work Colin." He forces a smile. "Now let's all go and be more efficient." He mechanically raises his arm and fist-pumps the air. "Maybe, I'll sit over—" He suddenly stops and dramatically raises his palm to his forehead as though he's suddenly been dropped into a poorly choreographed soap opera. "Oh, that's right," he says, enunciating each word. "Luckily I just remembered. I almost forgot that I have a... coffee catch up with... um... with... Karen," he says and races off towards the photocopy room, hoping he remembered correctly that that's where any items would be left.

"Enjoy you're coffee Boss," Colin waves and steps into the lift. "Oh, hey Mike the Intern." Colin says in surprise. "Aren't you getting off here?"

Mike quickly looks up from his phone. "Oops. Nearly did it again." He laughs and pushes himself off the back wall. "Oh, are you going for coffee?" he says pointing at Graham's cup. "Hold the lift for a sec and I'll come too." He takes two steps into the corridor and sees Colin's Notebook and pencil case in the distance. He slips his backpack off, swings his arm behind him and launches his bag out the doors. It bounces twice and slams into the wall directly opposite with a crunch.

"Ouch," Colin says. "I hope you don't have lunch in there. I think we can wait if you want to get your computer out of your locker and set up." He presses the Door Open button.

"No. I don't think we can," Graham grumbles, glaring at Mike.

"All good." Mike smiles. "I took my computer home with me; it's already in my backpack."

"I feel so bad for accidentally cutting in front of that man in the queue." Colin says, pushing the button for level 26.

"I don't think you can blame yourself mate," Graham says, stepping into the lift after him. "How were you to know he was in line? He was already drinking a coffee. It's a reasonable assumption that if

163

someone is already drinking coffee, they're probably not in the queue."

"I suppose," Colin scratches his ear as the doors close. "If he needed a coffee just to be able to get through queuing for *another* coffee, he probably does need to go first. I wish I'd been able to reach my cup in my locker though," he says take a sip from a paper cup with - Craven. - written on it.

"Hey," Mike says picking up his bag as they step out of the lift. "Who's that?" He points over towards Colin's desk.

They follow his finger over at a man in a tan suit sitting at the desk where he Graham had left his bag. "Excuse me mate," Graham says, walking up behind him. "You didn't notice a brown bag on this desk by any chance?" When there's no response, looks over his shoulder and sees he's on a video call. Graham taps him on the shoulder, then lifts his fingers to his ears and pulls them aways in the universal sign for - take your earphones out. "You see a brown bag here?" He looks at the name on the screen. "Richard?"

"One second," Richard says into his microphone. "There's someone interrupting at me." He turns to Graham. "Yes?"

Graham describes his bag and asks again if he happened to notice someone moving it.

"Oh that. I put it in the photocopy room," Richard says flatly and returns to his meeting.

Graham opens his mouth... but initially nothing comes out. He shakes his head to get things working again. "I'm sorry?" he says, wiggling his finger in his ear as though it must be blocked. "It sounded like you said - you put my bag in the photocopy room."

"Wait," Richard sighs to the screen again. "Yeah, he's still here." He half-turns. "Yes. That's what I said. It was abandoned."

Graham puts his coffee down. "How did you arrive at abandoned? I put it here to indicate that this is where I was going to sit," he says, folding his arms.

"How was I supposed to know that's what it meant?" Richard shrugs and turns back to his meeting again.

Graham looks blankly between him, Colin and Mike. "Uh. How would you know?" he says leaning onto the desk into Richard' line of sight. "I don't know, maybe societal rules? Common decency? Cultural evolution?"

"This desk is taken," Richard says without looking at him. "I'm already sitting here." He pushes his earphone back in. "What's the status on the Manchester account?"

Graham sucks a breath through his teeth and lets it out slowly. "I can see that, *Dick*. But I left my bag here to claim this desk, because this is where I'm planning to sit."

"One second," Richard huffs into his microphone. "I think he's trying to get me to move." He nods at the response from his meeting. "Yes, I've told him I'm already sitting here."

"Listen mate, you can move or I'll take that computer of yours and shove it up your—"

"Hey," Mike taps him on the shoulder. "Isn't that your bag?" He points to a Security Guard carrying a brown bag towards the lifts.

"Oh for Christsake," Graham gasps. "Hey!" he yells at the Guard stepping into the lift. "Hey, that's my bag!" He rushes along the corridor and arrives just as the doors close. He clenches his jaw and watches the floor indicator count down to Ground.

"Glad I didn't leave my bag in someone else's spot," Mike says and kicks his backpack to the desk next to Richard's. "I better get the rest of my stuff." He tips his computer and mouse onto the desk with a thunk. "Oh, dammit. I don't have my wireless keyboard. He glances over to the lift. "And my locker is one floor down." He snatches up his keys and wanders off towards the lift.

"Good luck," Colin says. His computer has finally started, he types in his password and presses enter. While he waits, he takes a breath and in his best ring-announcer voice says, "Let's get readyyyy.... to be more efficienttttt..."

"Do you mind?" Richard turns curtly. "I'm in a meeting."

"How's the new desk Colin?" Bob suddenly pops up from the other side of the cubicle wall.

"Boss!" Colin smiles. "Wow, I can't believe I'm sitting so close to the Commander." He looks around and whispers. "I think we've chosen the best desks. I'm glad I got here early."

"Yes," Bob nods trying to ease his fingernail under the edge of the bright orange - **Abandoned** - sticker on his laptop. "Quick or the dead."

"In a meeting." Richard glares at them.

"Who's he?" Bob asks. "I thought I saw Graham's bag there."

"So did I," Graham says walking up and dropping back on the desk next to Richard's computer.

"Taken," Richard says without looking up.

Bob looks at his watch. "It's nearly twenty past nine, are you saying you haven't even turned your computer on yet?"

"No seats," Graham says flatly.

Bob squints at him. "What do you mean?" he says.

"Oh, sorry," Graham shakes his head. "What did I say?"

"You said there were no seats."

"Right." Graham nods. "That's what I meant."

Bob rolls his eyes. "There can't be *no* seats."

Graham moves his arm in a wide arc to take in the entire floor. "There's. No. Seats," he says clearly. "Every desk is full."

"Maybe you should get here on time," Bob smirks and winks at Colin as though they are in some special 'in the know' club together.

"Actually, I was here *early*," Graham says and glares at Richard. "But some people don't understand how society works."

"He's back again," Richard says to his meeting. "No, I don't know why. I'm just ignoring him now."

"I don't know what you mean by no seats." Bob says in confusions as he scans the floor. "Surely there must be empty desks somewhere—"

"No seats," Gina says and drops her bag onto Colin's desk next to Graham's. "Doesn't make any sense." She scratches his head, looking around the full floor. "We only changed our desks. We still have the same number of people. Who's that?" she asks, suddenly noticing Richard.

"Don't get me started," Graham replies and perches back onto the edge of the desk. "I don't know who half these people are." He stares directly at Richard. "Or why they're taking up my space."

Colin looks around. "I'm surprised Poppy isn't here for our first day to make sure everything runs smoothly," he says pushing himself up in the chair to scan the area.

"I'd be more surprised if she *was* here," Graham snorts. "Any new initiative like this and the people behind it are always nowhere to be found."

"I see," Colin says and nods. "I suppose there'd be no need for Poppy to be here, because she'd be expecting everything to run smoothly."

"I can't find anywhere to sit..." Mike says, dropping his bag next to Gina's.

"Why are there no desks?" George huffs and adds his bag to the ever-expanding collection on Colin's desk. "And who are all these people?"

"I'll get to the bottom of this." Bob says and bangs his fist onto the desk softly. "I don't understand why there's no seats, but..." he pauses dramatically, and places his hands on his hips heroically, as though he's giving up the final space on last lifeboat on the Titanic. "You can take *my* spot."

"That's okay," Graham waves him away. "I'll find somewhere eventually," he says. "Even if it takes me all day."

"I wasn't talking to you," Bob says. "I was talking to Gina."

"I'm good," Gina says. "Anyone want coffee?"

Bob spins on his heel and strides away. "I'll go and speak to Poppy." He calls back to them over his shoulder. "I'll get to the bottom of this quick smart." He stabs at the lift button, mentally calculating how long it will take to get to the donut shop and back.

"I'm confused," Bob says, wiping some glaze off his sleeve.

Poppy sighs and rubs out the numbers on the whiteboard. She explains, again, the process the property team used to determine seating arrangements and team boundaries under the new flexi-desking regime.

"Yes, yes, I understand the process." Bob waves at her to stop. "I'm struggling with the logic..."

Poppy rubs the formula out again and begins to repeat the same monologue as the previous two times.

"Okay, look." Bob stands up. "I get that. What I *don't* get is why last week I had nine desks for my team, and now I have six. How do nine people work using six desks?"

"It's simple logistics," Poppy says as though she's having to explain to him that the reason it gets dark at night-time is because the sun has gone away.

"And how many days do they work from home?" Poppy smiles ready to deliver the final blow.

"Zero," Bob replies.

Poppy stops and opens her eyes wide. "Zero?"

"I'd love for them to work from home. Unfortunately, IT have been very clear that it's impossible to connect to the systems they use from outside of the office network." Bob shrugs innocently, not mentioning that the last time he raised the question was five years ago, and he hadn't asked again because he wasn't able to trust any of them to actually 'work' at home.

"Odd." Poppy frowns, tapping her chin. "They should be able to work from home."

"Out of my hands." Bob shrugs again. "Anyway, I don't see how any of this relates to the invasion of my Boundary and resulting lack of desks?"

Poppy turns back to the white board and scribbles another series of numbers and calculations. "Research shows that when you take into account the time that a staff member is not physically at their desk due to the meetings, leave, breaks etc we just discussed, that this equates to only a 70% desk utilisation over a given period." She steps back and clasps her hands together to show she is finished.

"And?" Bob rubs his forehead, trying to forestall an impending migraine.

Poppy looks at him blankly. "There is no 'and'. If our desks are occupied only 70% of the time, obviously you only need 70% of the capacity," she says, circling 70% to ensure Bob is following along. "We've reallocated the remaining wasted, empty time to other teams, giving us a 30% increase in efficiency." She puts her hands behind her back and bounces on the balls of her feet proudly, feeling like she has managed to explain the Theory of Relativity to a four-year-old.

"I not sure that's how it works," Bob frowns, unconvinced.

"Of course it does," Poppy retorts, forcing herself to not add – you idiot – to the end of her sentence. "When one staff member is away, another one simply utilises the vacant time at that desk."

Bob rubs his temple. "But my team's not; not using 30% of our allocated desks, 30% of the time. We're using *all* of them, *all* the time." Bob states.

Poppy turns back to the board and writes – Vacant Desk - in black marker. "Are there days when someone in your team isn't in the office because they're sick? Do they have holidays?" She writes them on the board without waiting for Bob to answer. "And they attend meetings?"

"Well, yes, of course they do," Bob says, feeling like he's the main suspect in a mystery movie. The chair suddenly feels uncomfortable and he shifts awkwardly. "But I don't really see the relevance—"

"Sick days." Poppy draws a thick circle around – Vacant Desk – on the board. "Holidays." She circles it again. "Meetings." Another circle.

"Okay, technically, that's true—"

"And they leave their desk to go to the toilet?" Poppy continues, cutting him off.

Bob shudders. "I hope so."

Poppy runs the marker around – Vacant Desk – again, and repeats each item on the list, adding another circle each time.

Bob moves his thumb towards his temple. "Yes, but the meetings they have are usually with each other. And with one or two exceptions, everyone takes leave at the same time during the enforced shutdown over Christmas. When you say that the desks aren't used 30% of the time. It's the same 30% of time for everyone. Also, my team don't alternate their toilet breaks like some kind of WrestleMania tag-team match."

"I don't really follow sports I'm afraid." Poppy holds her arms out apologetically and sits back in her chair.

"That's not my point." Bob leans forward, holding up his hands to show nine fingers. "What I'm saying is, that I have *nine* people–"

"Yes."

"Whose jobs require them to be *in* the office–"

175

"That's not particularly special," Poppy replies dismissively.

"Who are seated *at their desks* for 8 hours—"

"Minus breaks." Poppy interrupts, pointing to the board.

"Minus toilet breaks," Bob reluctantly agrees. "So..." He holds his hands out in the universal 'obviously that means' pose and waits for her to realise the dilemma.

"Was there anything else?" Poppy says, glancing at her watch.

Bob sits back and takes a deep breath. "If I have *nine* staff who *all* need to be in the office, and all need to be at their desks... *all* day, how do nine people do their work with only *six* desks?"

"The research is very clear." Poppy folds her arms and leans back in the chair to look down her nose at Bob.

"Okay," Bob sighs. "Maybe under laboratory conditions, or in some..." He waves his hands over his head. "Mystical theoretical universe, or possibly even for *other* teams that don't have staff whose entire job is to sit at their desk."

Poppy opens her phone and types as she talks. "I'll forward you the link to our intranet page which explains the research in more detail." She stops and lifts her hand up. "And while I'm sure you'll want to insist that I," she makes air quotes, "'do my own research', and 'think for myself', I'll happy to admit that I'm not clever enough to argue with science." Poppy finishes typing and presses send.

Bob presses his thumbs into his temples. "I think you're missing my point," he says to the floor.

"While I'm sure there are several online videos or experts you could forward me links to," Poppy replies, pushing herself out of the chair. "I'm sure if you set aside a few minutes to read the research, you'll see it's all about desk optimisation. A good leader is able to schedule their team's annual leave at different times. You said you had nine staff members? Simply schedule each person's leave for a different month, and you've found yourself an entire spare desk for most of the year right there."

Bob drags his fingers through his hair in frustration, and asks whether she feels it may be unfair to insist that his team take their leave at specific times for no other reason than to ensure an unbroken flow of desk-related vacancies.

"I don't see an issue," she replies.

Bob takes a breath and wonders whether he is the only sane person in the company. "Let's, for the sake of argument," he begins slowly. "Pretend that I asked my team to agree to the preposterous concept of a holiday roster. What about the other three months?"

Poppy does a quick mental calculation. "Everyone has an allocation of sick days," she responds. "Leaving a desk vacant. With nine staff, that totals more than the remaining time. And as you mentioned, there's the compulsory annual shutdown at the end of the year. It's beginning to sound to me like you've got too many desks."

"But *everyone* is on leave then!" Bob exclaims. "If they are all on leave *then*, how can they go on leave during the year?"

"Checkmate Atheists," Vanessa says as Bob finishes recounting his meeting with Poppy to the team.

"You sure told her." Umi smiles. "Thanks for sticking up for us Bob."

"Is that what *actually* happened?" Graham squints and moves out of the way of someone trying to use the microwave. "And why are we meeting in the kitchen?"

"That's the way I remember it," Bobs replies quickly, not mentioning that in reality the entire Property team had taken the week off to avoid dealing with any fallout. And that when he had eventually been able to get a hold of Poppy on her mobile, she had simply read the information on the intranet page to him word for word and finished up with a curt - *That's the policy, and it applies to everyone.*

"Yay for the Boss!" Colin says and reaches forward to give him a high-five.

"Good," Gina says rubbing her back. "Does that mean we get our desks back tomorrow? I'm stuck at the rickety table over there." She points to a white plastic table in the corner, with a stack of napkins under one leg.

179

"I can't say." Bob holds out his hands apologetically. "My hands are tied."

Gina glances at Bob's hands.

"Metaphorically," he says, putting them behind his back. "I've escalated it to Senior Management. I'm afraid that's all I can do for the moment. I've forwarded each of you the link to Property's intranet page, and the research." He steps aside to let someone get to the hot water tap.

"It says here that desks are available on a first come, first served basis," Umi says scrolling the page.

"That's correct." Bob nods. "Poppy said that we could arrive thirty minutes early to secure a desk if we wanted to," he says, recalling what he had read on the intranet.

"Sorry, I need to get to the fridge."

"Oh, no problem." Bob steps out of the way.

Gina raises her hand. "But then won't other people start coming in thirty-five minutes early to get here before us..." She pauses and rubs her lower back. "And then we'd have to come in *forty* minutes early..."

Graham laughs. "Maybe we should just set up a campsite."

"Great idea!" Colin smiles. "That sounds like fun!"

Vanessa looks over to Bob. "Can't *you* just get here half an hour early and secure the desks for us?"

Bob takes a step back and folds his arms dramatically. "I said that to them." He scowls and shakes his head strongly to show how unbelievable the conversation had been. "I *said* to them," he repeats and bangs his fist into the palm of his hand. "I said that I'm prepared to throw myself on the grenade and come in early to secure the area for my troops—"

"What, are we in the Army now?" Gina interrupts.

"I believe," Bill rubs his chin. "You'll find that actually *isn't* the case about the grenades," he says. "Although I did have one Commander, Captain Three-fingers Johnson—"

"That's very nice of you to come in early to save a desk for us." Umi smiles.

Bob shakes his head in what is intended to show disgust, but looks more like a dog that's just fallen into a pond. "Unfortunately, I can't," he says. "I'm," he makes air quotes. "'not allowed to.' Because it would be..." He lifts his fingers again, "'against company policy', and would result in," his uses air quotes for a third time, "'disciplinary action. Up to, and including termination of employment.'" He swallows. "Now, don't get me wrong. *I'm* not afraid *to* fight that fight..." He puffs out his chest and stares off into the middle distance. "That's a hill I'm prepared to die on," he says bravely. Safe in the knowledge that this is a battle that will never be waged.

"Make up your mind then," Brenda glares at him. "Are you saying you're coming in early for us or not? I can't spend all day here. I've got things to do," she huffs. "Those hot dogs aren't going to wrap themselves."

"I just told you," Bob sighs. "I can't—" he stops and turns suddenly to Brenda. "*Hot dogs to wrap?*" Before she can answer he holds up a hand to stop her. "No," he says. "I don't want to know." He closes his eyes for a moment and thinks about donuts, then looks back to the group. "Anyway, as I was saying," he forces a heavy sigh, as though he's volunteering for a behind the enemy lines mission that will result in certain doom. "To help *you*..." He looks at each person in turn. "I'm prepared to work from home, whenever I'm able to." He opens his arms magnanimously. "And I'm prepared to do this to ensure that *you...* my team... aren't forced to deal with uncomfortable work areas." He shakes his head again in an attempt to display frustration, but it comes across more like he's thinks he has a bug crawling up his neck.

"That's very admirable of you," a man holding up a container of food says. "Can I get to the fridge please?"

"Not that I have a decent set up at home," Bob says, stepping aside. "It will probably be worse than that rickety table of yours over there Gina." He attempts an ironic laugh and nods at her. "But that's what a good leader does." He places his hands on his hips, stands tall and gazes off into the middle distance heroically.

"If your place is worse, then wouldn't you be better off coming into the office and sitting at the rickety table, and let me work from home," Gina counters.

"Let's not get down into the weeds today," Bob interrupts quickly. "Don't worry, we'll get through this..." he pauses. "As a team." To add gravity to his message, he makes meaningful eye contact with each one of them. Which just ends up creating a long uncomfortable silence. "Let's try and be here early, as

Poppy recommends. In a worst-case scenario, perhaps some of you can alternate between a desk and one of the temporary, short term, non-bookable desks."

"I think you mean *broken* desks..." Vanessa says. "Like Gina's one over there."

"That's not my desk!" Gina snaps. "If I have to sit there too much longer, I'll be on Worker's Comp."

"Tell me again how this is increasing engagement?" Graham says.

"You're overthinking things," Bob jumps in. "Let's get back to work, and we'll deal with this, the way we deal with *every* difficult situation—"

"Ignore it?"

"What? No." Bob slaps his forehead. "I meant with *resilience*, and *gall* and—"

"Other trite platitudes," Gina grumbles and limps off. "Meanwhile, I'm still stuck in this Centre for Disease Control we jokingly call a kitchen."

"Wait, why are *you* sitting here? Didn't I give up my desk for you this morning?" Bob looks at her quizzically.

"I thought you were giving it to Graham," she says.

"I thought you were giving it to Mike." Graham shrugs.

"My neighbour's cat stares at me through the window," Mike says, picking at something under his fingernail.

"I—" Bob glances at Mike and blinks. "What?" He shakes his head to clear it. "No, I gave it to Gina, because she's a girl."

"Because I'm a *what?*" Gina spins back, the volume in her voice rising.

"You know what I mean." Bob tries to say casually, pulling at his collar. "I was just being polite."

"You can be polite without implying that because I'm female, I'm somehow more needy of your precious desk than a lazy, fat, stupid, old man."

"I don't think Graham's *that* old," Mike says supportively.

Graham raises an eyebrow at him. "Yeah, well at least I've never set fire to a photocopier," he says.

"Hey!" Mike yelps indignantly, insulted at the injustice of Graham's comment. "Besides, the third time wasn't even my fault."

"Alright, that's enough." Bob stops them. "Gina," he says. "If you want to sit at my desk so you don't have to go back to the rickety table over there, you're welcome to it." He holds up a hand before she can speak. "If you *don't*, then feel free to pass it on to someone else." He snaps his computer shut and steps towards the door. "Now let's get back to work."

"Yes!" Colin checks his watch. "We've still got three more hours of efficiency left for the day." He bounces off the chair and follows the team back out into the corridor.

"I'll have the desk if you don't want it Gina," Mike says. "I'm sitting on the floor in here," he says, peeling off into the utility room. "Smells funny, but you get used to the headache after a while."

The other continue back to their space. Pooja stops. "This place all looks the same," she says, looking around to check her location. "Wait, I remember that cat poster," she says, confirming she's in the right place. ""Uh, excuse me," she says to a woman, who is sitting at Pooja's desk. "I think you're in my chair."

"Desk was empty," the woman says, without looking up from her computer.

"It wasn't *empty*," Pooja starts. "All my equipment was here—" she looks at the desk. "Why are all my things on the floor?"

"Policy is," the woman continues, still focused on her computer. "That if you're away for more than thirty minutes you need to pack up your things so someone else can use the desk."

"But I wasn't *away* for more than thirty minutes..." Pooja says politely. "I was in a meeting—"

The woman shrugs disinterestedly. "I don't make the rules," she says and continues typing.

"I need to talk to my manager." Pooja frowns and walks over to Bob. "Someone's sitting at my desk," she says, pointing back at the woman.

"And someone's sitting at *my* desk," George grumbles walking up.

Vanessa appears, joining the group. "And there's a guy from sales sitting at *my* desk,"

Colin sits up in his chair and wriggles his fingers. "And his porridge is toooo colllld," He giggles.

"I think it's too late in the day to be eating porridge," Bill says checking his watch.

Graham leans over. "I think he meant like Goldilocks..." he stops as he sees Bill tap his watch to make sure it's working. "Never mind."

Alfred appears from behind a cluster of chairs, balancing a clipboard and a frazzled expression. "Who's got time for porridge?" he complains. "I've just found all my equipment in the utility room!"

In the distance a voice that sounds like a train derailment slices through the background hum of the office. "Where are my hot dogs!" Brenda screams at a cowering security guard, as he frantically presses the lift button to escape.

"Gosh," Colin says. "I'm beginning wonder whether this initiative *is* increasing our engagement and efficiency as much as Poppy had hoped for. It doesn't seem very efficient to have to move every half an hour." He notices a movement out of the corner of his eye. Hey, there's someone at *my* desk!" he gasps, then stops and corrects himself. "Well, not *my* desk, but my new flexi-desk."

"Okay," Bob pushes his thumb into his temple. "Let's just get through the rest of this afternoon and I'll see if I can get Poppy on another call."

The team gather around Bob's laptop as Poppy joins the meeting. "I understand your team are still confused with the policy?" she says, adjusting her camera.

"You're going to have to speak up," Graham says. "We can't hear you."

The team squeezes in more tightly. Colin turns his head so his ear is closer to the speaker,

"Why are you in the kitchen?" Poppy asks, moving closer to the camera.

"What did she say?" Bill asks, raising his hand to his ear.

"Don't lean on the table," Gina says to Bob, pushing her foot against the leg. "The whole thing will tip over."

"Why aren't you in a meeting room?" Poppy continues her line of questioning.

Bob explains that all the meeting rooms have been taken over by people using them to work, because there's not enough desks. And that now that *his* team have lost *their* desks, so they're all crammed into the kitchen, at the rickety table that's Gina's desk.

"It's not my desk!" Gina protests again.

"I see," Poppy says.

"What did she say?" Brenda calls out from the back. "Can you ask her where my hot dogs are?"

"She said – I see," George turns to repeat it over his shoulder.

"Sees what?" Brenda snaps. "What does she see?" She folds her arms tightly. "She doesn't see my hot dogs, that's for sure," she snorts.

After five minutes of misheard conversation, interspersed with 'what did she say?' Bob decides that it's best for the others to sit off to the side and let him handle it.

"If you believe there is a potential desk deficit," Poppy says, when everyone has calmed down. "Then the simplest answer is to work alternating days remotely."

"I've offered to do that," Bob says.

"You'll need to speak up," Poppy replies, pushing her headphone tightly onto her ear. "What's that noise?"

Bob leans in close to the microphone. "Suzanne from Accounts is having a work anniversary," Bob yells over the clapping coming from the table next to them.

"Five years!" Colin calls over from next to Suzanne, and takes another bite of cake. "Oops," he says. "I think I need to get back to the team." He jumps off the chair. "Congratulations, and thank you for the cake." He waves.

Graham walks over behind Bob and leans forward to the screen. "Sorry, are you saying *I* have to work from home?"

Poppy shakes her head. "I'm not saying it's mandatory. If you'd prefer to be in the office—"

"I don't imagine that's the case." Bob interrupts sneering at Graham.

"Oh yeah," Graham agrees. "I'm definitely okay not coming into the office. What I'm asking is - do I have to be *at home*? As in, can I work remotely from somewhere else?"

"Do you mean, like your partner's home?" Poppy asks.

"Nah, I was thinking more of you know, a coffee shop, or..." He waves his hands vaguely.

"I'm not sure that would be viable for a full day," Poppy says, "Perhaps for an hour or two. Do you have a local cafe you like to go to?"

"No, not really," Graham says wistfully. "Nothing specific, just checking, you know, Cafe, common area, pub—"

"You can't work from a pub Graham," Bob interrupts. "You shouldn't even need to be told that."

Graham holds out his hands innocently. "I'm not saying I would. It's just an example."

"I think there would be too many distractions in a bar," Poppy says.

"I agree," Bob glares at Graham. "Far too disruptive."

"Sorry, I missed that," Poppy says. "I couldn't hear you over the people singing Happy Birthday." She puts her finger onto the headphone again. "But I would suggest developing a schedule where you work alternate days remotely to be able to gain the most value from this innovative use of our space."

"I don't see how wobbly tables are an innovative anything," Gina says, returning back to the conversation.

"Maybe it would be best if we *all* work from home for a few days," Alfred suggests, shouldering his way into Bob's camera view. "Then we can all get used to it together. That way we can help each other with any problems."

"A team building activity!" Colin pumps his paw into the air. "Great idea Alfred!"

"Good idea." Poppy nods. "An example of how working remotely brings people together."

"Brings people together..." Bob sighs and resigns himself to the situation. "By having them all work from different places."

"Okay, I'm glad it's been such a success for you." Poppy smiles and ends the meeting before anyone can add anything else.

Bob stares at the blank screen. "Right," he says flatly and closes his laptop.

"I think we should be able to leave early and get set up for tomorrow." Gina says, rubbing her foot. "It's impossible to get anything done sitting here. Oh. Thank you Suzanne," she says taking a piece of cake. "We may as well go to the pub."

"I'm with Gina," Mike says. "Also, Security said they aren't comfortable with me being alone in the photocopy room. I just need to put my computer and everything in my locker and I'll meet you downstairs."

"What do you mean put your computer in your locker?" Bob pushes a thumb into his temple "You need to take it with you. How else are you going to work from home?"

Pooja picks up her keyboard and mouse from the pile next to the table on the floor. "Do I need to take these as well?"

"Good question," agrees George.

Bob looks between them. "Do you *have* a keyboard and mouse at home?"

Pooja furrows her brow as she considers it for a moment. "No," she says. "I don't think so."

"I don't," George shakes his head firmly. "The only time I really use a computer is for work."

Bob leans forward slightly. "And do you use your keyboard and mouse in the office?"

"Oh all the time." George agrees. "I couldn't survive without them."

"Yeah. same here," chimes in Pooja.

"So, if you couldn't survive without them..." Bob looks between them slowly, hoping they'll put two and two together "And you *don't* have one at home..." He waves his hand in a circle to encourage them to answer.

George lifts his keyboard and hovers it over his bag. "So... do we..."

"Yes," Bob snaps. "Yes, take them with you." He turns to the others. "Anything you would usually use in the office, take it home with you."

"But I've already got a mouse and keyboard at home," Vanessa says. "Why would I need two?"

Bob pushes his thumb into his temple again. "If you've already got a keyboard and mouse at home, then *don't* take them from the office."

"Oh," Alfred says pulling his keyboard out of his bag.

"And what about this?" Bill asks.

Bob rubs his forehead and stares at the object in Bill's hand. "Are you seriously asking if you need to take the power cable for your computer?"

"Didn't have things like this in my day you know," Bill says. "Back in my day—"

"Electricity hadn't been invented yet," Gina snorts.

"Sorry, I missed that," George says. "Was that a yes or no to the cable?"

"Yes, you need to take the power cable!" Bob drops his head into his hands as Brenda, Umi and Vanessa open their bags again and add their cables.

"I think I've got one of these at home," Pooja holds her cable up.

"Take it just in case." Bob pushes his thumb further into his temple and feels his shoulders begin to relax.

Colin checks his bag and makes sure he has his computer, all his cables, his mouse and special keyboard. "It's going to be fun to work from home." He smiles.

Brenda looks over at him. "Don't you live in a tree?" she asks, stuffing two boxes of twenty-four pens, six A4 notepads, and four staplers into her bag.

Colin frowns. "No, I live in the Eucalyptus apartments near the river," he says, and wonders if he should be hoarding stationery as well.

"Oh," Brenda says, pushing a stack of yellow folders into her backpack. "I just thought that was the name you gave your tree." She holds up her power cable. "Did we need this or not?"

‎

The next morning, Colin jumps out of bed, excited to try working from home. He smiles to himself, remembering the survey meeting and all the people working virtually on the screen. The lady who had reminded him of Mrs Magpie's babies, the man with the giant clown painting, and the red-bearded man playing charades.

He showers and combs his fur, dresses in the blue work suit he had laid out for himself the night before, and hangs his security pass around his neck. "Ready to roll." He gives himself a thumbs up in the mirror and steps into the dining room to the special area he had designated as his office. He moves the bowl of fruit to the right-side of the dining table, and turns on his computer. While he's waiting for it to go through it's ten-minute start up cycle, he turns around and straightens the new sign he had made that reads - 'Colin's Office'.

He sits down and adjusts his Special Reminder Notebook to make sure it's aligned with the computer, and takes a sip from the fresh cup of coffee steaming on the table.

When his computer has finished starting up, he checks his email he received yesterday for the instructions on how to connect to the company network from home. At the bottom he sees details for how to contact the Help Desk in the event there is a problem. He keeps his claws crossed that everything runs smoothly, and is pleasantly surprised when the entire process takes less than five minutes. He wonders why Bob had always told the team that logging in from home was far too complicated, and technical for any of them to be able to do.

"Colin Koala reporting for duty." He salutes, and glances at his watch.

Quarter to seven.

"That doesn't seem right." He scratches his ear and walks over to checks the big clock in the kitchen. It also says quarter to seven. "How weird," Colin says to himself and then realises he'd forgotten to take into account the hour and a half of travel it would usually take for him to get to the office.

He sits back down. "Well, I'm ready to work, so I may as well be productive," he says and spends the next hour tidying and organising all his files. He even manages to categorise his emails, archive the ones he no longer needs, and unsubscribe from the update alerts and newsletters he had thought were a good idea when he started, but has never opened.

With a final flourish, he reads the last email in his inbox, and watches the Unread total drop to zero.

He leans back and smiles proudly. It's not even nine o'clock yet, and he's more organised than he's been for months. "Looks like it's organisation central at Colin's Office." He smiles and winks at the sign over his shoulder.

He checks his watch again. Still twenty-five minutes till start time. "Maybe another coffee?" he says thoughtfully. "In case it becomes a busy day."

He pours himself a fresh cup, and sends Graham a message on Chatter, to say good morning.

He watches the cursor flash, and after five minutes realises that Graham is showing as off-line. He hopes he isn't having any troubles setting his computer up.

He checks to see if anyone else is online, and says 'Hi' to Pooja. She sends him an emoji saying hi, and he returns with a gif of a cat waving hello. They alternate swapping memes a few minutes, and then she suddenly goes off-line. He hopes everything is okay with her too.

He checks his watch again and sees he still has ten minutes until the weekly stand-up begins.

He remembers how it used to be a *daily* stand-up. But after the first week, everyone had complained it was pointless and boring, because they were all just repeating the same things as the day before. When Graham suggested only having a Stand-Up when someone had something to say, everyone had agreed, but Bob had insisted they had to meet at least once a week anyway.

Bing! goes the reminder for the Stand-Up, and Colin clicks on the link to join. He checks that his camera captures his new 'Colin's Office' sign behind him, and waits patiently for the others to arrive. He's excited to be able to see everyone else's 'home office,' and scribbles a few doodles in his Special Reminder Notebook while he waits.

A few minutes after nine, George pops up on the screen with a loud Ding!

Colin waves and starts to say hello, but every time he tries to speak, he's interrupted by another loud Ding! when a new person joins.

Vanessa appears on the screen in a t-shirt and baseball cap, Umi looks like she is in her dressing gown. Alfred has on a blue cardigan, the same colour as Colin's suit.

When Gina appears, she's sideways, and it takes Colin a few seconds to work out that it's because she is lying in bed with the computer next to her. Her hair droops across her face and she pulls a Ferris Bueller's Day off blanket up to her chin.

"Hey Gina." Colin waves to her. "Cool blanket."

Gina's eyes burst open, and she slams the computer closed. Colin watches her status blink and change to 'offline'.

"What's going on with this thing now?" The top of Graham's head appears on the screen as he fiddles with something under the table. "Useless piece of... Why are you doing *that*? Oh for fuc—"

"You're not on mute Graham," Colin jumps in quickly.

Graham's eyes pop up above the table. He ducks down again and there's a loud thump. "Jesus Christ!" he yells and appears again from under the desk, rubbing his head. "I can't believe," he pushes himself slowly off the floor. "That in an era where a crazy billionaire can put an electric car into space; that I still have to crawl around on the floor to plug in a freaking power cable." He touches his head lightly. "Ow. There's a lump."

"Oh, were we supposed to bring the cable home?" Bill asks.

"Team," Bob appears on screen.

"Morning boss." Colin waves.

Bob waves back and scans his screen. "Where's Gina?" he asks. "Graham," he says rolling his eyes. "Can you change your shirt please?"

Graham leans back. "What?" he asks and pulls the shirt taut across his chest. It reads - 'Senior Management... Putting the 'N' in 'CUTS'.

"I'd prefer not to have to talk to Harold in HR again for a while," Bob says. "So if you could change your shirt to something more appropriate."

Graham sighs and puts his hands on the table to push himself out of the chair.

"Stop!" Bob yells before Graham can move.

Graham huffs. "Now what?" He throws his arms up.

Bob leans forward and squints at the screen. "Are you wearing pants?"

Graham looks down. "What do you mean?"

"Just turn your camera off for now." Bob rubs his forehead. "In future, can everyone *please* check what you're wearing before you join." He shakes his head. "And that includes pants. *Thank* you."

Colin makes a note in his Special Reminder notebook about how Bob always has such good manners. Even sometimes when he's a little annoyed he always says 'please' and 'thank you.'

Graham's picture disappears as Gina's pops up again. Her hair is pulled back into a tight ponytail, and she's sitting in her kitchen.

"Okay everyone," Bob begins. "Is everyone set up? No problems or issues?"

"With this?" Graham asks. "Or just generally?"

"Let's stick with this for now," Bob says. "And can you please keep yourself on mute if you're not talking Graham," Bob says.

"I *was* talking," Graham replies. "That's why I wasn't on mute."

"And whoever's eating toast." Bob rubs his forehead. "Can you also— You know what; everyone – just put yourself on mute," he snaps. "Now does anyone have any problems or concerns that they want to raise..." He sees Graham's status switch off mute. "Specifically, about working from home," he adds quickly.

Graham's status changes back.

Bob waits for a few seconds. He had been expecting a barrage of complaints, but is pleasantly surprised when there's silence. He wonders for a moment if perhaps he has underestimated the situation, and whether the team *is* taking this seriously after all. "Alright then," he says and notices Colin pointing at the bottom of the screen.

Bob clicks the blinking chat icon and the window fills with scrolling text. "What the—" He jumps back. "What's all this?" he gasps as the mass of text continues to scroll past.

George un-mutes himself and says quickly. "You told us all to go on mute." And mutes himself again.

"Okay, okay. Stop typing." Bob takes a deep breath. "Is any of... this..." he points at the screen. "Work related concerns or problems?"

"Yes!" They all come off mute at once, causing him to jump back.

Bob lifts a finger for them to wait. "Problems that will stop you from doing your work today? Unmute yourself *only* if you have an issue that will *stop you* doing your job." He tenses his shoulders and waits.

After thirty seconds of silence. He checks that the chat function is still working, which is also quiet. He waits a few more seconds, confirms he is still connected to the internet and continues. "Okay," he says. "Let's begin the meeting. Who would like to go first? Does anyone have any thoughts about working from home?"

"Does anyone know why my computer battery is low?" Bill scratches his head.

Bob stares over at his liquor cabinet, and pushes a thumb into his temple. "Anyone else?"

Colin throws his hand up in the air. "I do! I was already excited about increasing my efficiency by flexi-desking in the office. And this morning I confirmed that the further I am from my original desk... the more efficient I become! Flexi-desking has been an amazing initiative." Colin smiles and sits back comfortably. "I'm so pleased I could be a part of it."

"Thank you for your continued support Colin," Bob says relaxing a little. "Any other comments?" He sees Brenda squint and leans forward towards the screen. Her face comes so close enough to the camera that everyone can see the hairs poking out of her nose.

"Hey!" She suddenly leans back and stabs her finger at the screen. "How come Colin gets an office and we don't?" says, pointing at his sign,

Bob blinks twice and sits silently. He hears the tick-tock of the clock behind him. "Let's finish up the meeting for today," he says, zombie-like, and leans forward to slide the cover over his camera. "We'll talk later." He glances over towards his liquor cabinet again.

"Great meeting Boss." Bob hears Colin say as he mindlessly closes the lid of his laptop. "Finished early! Extra efficient!"

Thank You!

I hope you enjoyed reading **Colin Doesn't Call the Help Desk** as much as I enjoyed writing them (at least as much as I enjoyed it during the first fourteen edits). If you did, you'll also enjoy Book 1: <u>Colin Calls the Help Desk</u> – Available on Amazon.

Colin would also be very excited if you could give him a review. It makes him feel good, and helps others discover how to add value, step up and lean in, without falling over. If you enjoy typing website addresses into your browser, this URL will take you straight to the review page:

<u>https://www.amazon.com/review/create-review?&asin=B0CW1BYDRX</u>

Otherwise, it' probably easier to jump onto the book's page on Amazon and scroll down.

You're a legend!

Cheers

Elwood
<u>https://elwoodscott.com</u>

Acknowledgements

When I amazed myself by eventually completing Colin Calls the Help Desk, I had plans for a Colin Book Two, but was never quite sure I would finish it.

Firstly, thank you again to Mitch Pleasance for the amazing job of creating the illustration of Colin. Mitch is also the guy who did my typewriter tattoo. If you're looking for a good tattoo, Mitch is your man. You can find him on Instagram - @mitchpleasance

Thank you to everyone who read, reviewed and provided useful and beneficial feedback. It has all made a difference to how this book turned out.

Pallavi, for your helpful comments, and for laughing at my jokes.

Louise, thank you for your feedback, comments and ongoing support.

My podcast buddy Scott for being a sounding board again, for providing advice and support on content and on the cover design. And for helping to build my social media presence, despite my inconsistent involvement.

Thanks Liam again for cover support, and Eb for being my cheer squad.

Thanks to Psychostick, Devil Driver, Elmer Bernstein, Kiss, Alice Cooper, and Devin Townsend for the background music while I was writing.

And thank you to all the people who were there in the beginning and helped to shape Colin into the Koala he is today.

www.ingramcontent.com/pod-product-compliance
Ingram Content Group UK Ltd.
Pitfield, Milton Keynes, MK11 3LW, UK
UKHW020707180925
7959UKWH00019B/265

9 780645 052480